GREAT QUESTIONS IN POLITICS SERIES

Globalization and State Power

Who Wins When America Rules?

D1514916

JOEL KRIEGER

WELLESLEY COLLEGE

PEARSON
Longman

New York   San Francisco   Boston
London   Toronto   Sydney   Tokyo   Singapore   Madrid
Mexico City   Munich   Paris   Cape Town   Hong Kong   Montreal

To Carol, Nathan, and Megan—

this time, more than ever.

—————

Executive Editor:	Eric Stano
Senior Marketing Manager:	Elizabeth Fogarty
Production Manager:	Denise Phillip
Project Coordination, Text Design, and Electronic Page Makeup:	WestWords, Inc.
Cover Design Manager:	John Callahan
Cover Designer:	Kay Petronio
Cover Art:	Courtesy PictureQuest
Senior Manufacturing Buyer:	Alfred C. Dorsey
Printer and Binder:	Phoenix Color Corporation
Cover Printer:	Phoenix Color Corporation

Library of Congress Cataloging-in-Publication Data

Krieger, Joel, 1951–
  Globalization and state power : who wins when America rules? / Joel Krieger.
    p. cm.
  ISBN 0-321-15968-3
  1. Globalization. 2. National state. 3. Power (Social sciences) 4. United States—
Relations—Foreign countries. I. Title.

  JZ1318.K75 2005
  327.73—dc22

                              2004021285

Please visit our website at http://www.ablongman.com

ISBN 0-321-15968-3

1 2 3 4 5 6 7 8 9 10—PHH—07 06 05 04

Contents

Preface

As globalization has become the watchword of our age, it seems that the famous aphorism of Tip O'Neill, the garrulous Massachusetts Democrat and Speaker of the House during the Carter and Reagan presidencies, "all politics is local," has been turned upside down. Trade and investment crisscrossing the globe, mass migration, cultural diffusion, internationally negotiated or imposed limits to the sovereignty of states: none of this is unprecedented. But the density, speed, variety, and scope of cross-border connections in the contemporary world are unique.

Has all politics become global? Of course not, but the question helps frame an agenda for investigating how politics and power at the level of the nation-state are shaped by globalization. Tip O'Neill's boastful maxim underscored the simple fact that success at national politics meant cutting the deals and securing the bases of political support at home. In a similar vein, this book stakes the claim that the very capacity of states to exercise power effectively (which can make or break success in national politics) hinges on the ability of governments to manage the challenges of globalization successfully.

It is a motivating premise of this book that globalization marks an historic juncture in global politics: globalization reframes both the role and function of states in the global order and how we understand their role and function. This book analyzes how globalization recasts state power in a global order in which the United States exerts preeminent power and hence largely shapes the institutions and sets the agenda of global politics.

DEFINING GLOBALIZATION

Before embarking on this analysis, it is necessary to first clarify the frame of reference. What do we mean by globalization? This is a deceptively complicated question and every attempt at an answer has become very contested.

As if acting out the Buddhist parable of the blind men and the elephant, some observers focus on only one element. Globalization is colonization or spatial reorganization or the creation of a single world society or Americanization or deterritorialization or the liberalization of markets. Other definitions are very general: globalization refers very broadly to "the process of increasing interconnectedness between societies such that events in one part of the world have effects on peoples and societies far away."[1]

Our definition of globalization recognizes the scope of the processes associated with globalization, yet it takes a position that globalization produces both winners and losers, and it focuses the definition on politics explicitly.

1. Scope. Globalization refers to the increasing scale, extent, variety, speed, and magnitude of cross-border social, economic, military, political, and cultural interactions.

2. Empirical proposition. Both the benefits and costs of globalization are unevenly distributed. Globalization therefore tends to produce paradoxical results. It fosters both growing interconnectedness and intensified animosities, driven by the prospect of expanding economic opportunities for some, yet exclusion and marginalization for others. Hence globalization is a contradictory phenomenon, one often experienced by ordinary citizens (and also by governments, grassroots activists, and officials in international organizations) as unsettling and full of risk.[2]

3. Definitional funnel. As broad in scope as the bundle of phenomena associated with globalization may be, in *Globalization and State Power* the definition will be narrowed in focus to encompass primarily the political, political-economic, and geopolitical domain.*

With this definition in place, the focus of the study comes easily into view.

THE PURPOSE AND PLAN OF THE BOOK

The shelves of bookstores are littered with books on *globalization*. But there are surprisingly few sustained efforts to focus specifically on *globalization and state power*. This book is intended to fill that gap by addressing two critical and interlocking questions:

1. How does globalization (and in particular, the global challenges of economic competitiveness, geopolitical influence, and security from terror attacks) affect state power understood as the capacity of states to secure desirable outcomes and influence the behavior of other states, transnational actors and international organizations?

2. What are the consequences of America's exercise of hegemonic power—for the capacity of other states to exercise power, for the shape of the geopolitical order, and for the United States itself?

---

*This definitional focus will be widened selectively to consider the role of cultural identity in global politics—and in the key debates that have framed our understanding of globalization and state power. Culture and identity will be considered, for example, in discussing Samuel Huntington's "class of civilizations" argument, when analyzing the political repercussions of Islam in French politics and in the debate over Turkish entry to the European Union, and in analyzing the religious and cultural fault lines that run through the political landscape in Iraq in the aftermath of war.

The daunting challenges of the post-9/11 era endow these core questions (and a set of subsidiary questions identified below) with particular urgency.

Until the terror attacks of September 11, 2001, the theme that promised to dominate the political agenda of the early twenty-first century was whether globalization would promote increased human development spread more evenly across the globe or reinforce the comparative advantages of the North against the South, undermine local cultures, and intensify regional conflicts. Since 9/11, everyone's attention has shifted to the problem of how America and the world can—and must—meet the security threats posed by terror networks and the states that harbor them and the implications of a new geopolitical order shaped by the hard power of what many are considering a new American empire.[3] *Globalization and State Power* analyzes this transformed global agenda and investigates how—and how successfully—states manage and absorb the repercussions of the immensely complex and inevitably destabilizing processes of globalization.

Does globalization necessarily lead to the declining authority of states and a "one size fits all" style of minimalist neoliberal politics (free markets, free trade, welfare retrenchment, and an attractive investment climate as the end game of every state's politics)? Do powerful transnational and intergovernmental institutions of global governance such as the World Trade Organization, the United Nations, and the International Monetary Fund help stabilize and govern an unruly world order—or create more problems than they resolve? Does America's unrivaled power in the world mean that it can go it alone—or suggest, more than ever, the need for constructive and cooperative relations with a vast array of countries in order to provide both security and stability?

THREE THESES ON GLOBALIZATION AND STATE POWER

The book is dedicated to a careful investigation of the interactive effects of globalization and state power. In *Globalization and State Power* readers will find answers to each of the questions posed above. In fact, in many cases you will find alternative answers inspired by powerful competing perspectives. The arguments developed in the book will culminate in three theses on globalization and state power, which speak directly to the two core questions that animate this study.

1. *The invisible hand thesis.* Thesis 1 emphasizes the economic advantages to the United States that follow from the global economic architecture and argue that globalization sustains American power at the expense of other states.
2. *The contested sovereignty of the state thesis.* Thesis 2 argues that globalization does not uniformly or implacably weaken states, but that globalization intensifies interstate negotiations. Globalization therefore reduces the autonomous capacity of all states (even the United States), and therefore

raises questions about the effectiveness and longevity of the American "empire."

3. *The globalization as the engine of democracy and progress thesis.* Thesis 3 contends that globalization spurs the expansion of market economies and the growth of a cross-border entrepreneurial middle-class, thereby challenging the sway of authoritarian regimes and fostering an international order recast in America's image and supporting its values.

It is hoped that the engagement with these powerful competing theses will inspire readers to debate along with the experts and come to their own conclusions, better informed about the issues and more cognizant about what is at stake in the positions they are prepared to defend as their own.

WHAT THIS BOOK IS . . . AND IS NOT

Caveat lector. This book will not take up every intriguing question about globalization! *Globalization and State Power* is not designed to be a comprehensive study of the full scope of globalization or a multidisciplinary introduction to global studies that would integrate the contributions of anthropology, sociology, geography, and cultural studies within an analysis of globalization. Instead, in thematic and disciplinary terms, *Globalization and State Power* is, first and foremost, a book about how globalization shapes the role and function of states—and how states, in turn, can (and cannot) act to bend the external political environment to their advantage. It focuses on national economic and social models, key geopolitical intrigues, and the daunting security challenges of the post-9/11 global order. It is also limited in geographical scope: core case studies are limited to the United States, EU Europe (especially Britain, Germany, and France), and East Asia (with particular emphasis on the response of the Asian Tigers to the economic crisis of 1997).

Because the United States enjoys disproportionate power and influence in shaping the economic, geopolitical, military, and political-cultural dimensions of globalization, the second core argument of the book analyzes American influence and critically assesses its consequences for the global order. But *Globalization and State Power* is not an American politics book. Rather, the arguments of this book are at the crossroads of comparative politics and international relations, located at the heavily trafficked intersection where domestic politics and international affairs cross paths. It preserves a focus on politics and political economy, broadly defined, with states as the primary unit of analysis.

OVERVIEW OF THE BOOK

Chapter 1 defines the baseline challenges to the exercise of state power in a global era. No state, even the most powerful, can secure desirable outcomes autonomously. Hence, the traditional concept of *sovereignty,* understood as the exclusive authority of a state within its territorial boundaries, has been rendered obsolete. In the introductory chapter we examine *multi-level governance* and argue that even more than the intensification of world trade or investment, this emerging framework of overlapping, incomplete, and competing sovereignties captures the defining feature of the contemporary global age.

In this introductory chapter, we also present a set of four high-profile interpretations of globalization or global politics (those of Thomas Friedman, Samuel Huntington, Joseph Stiglitz, and John Mearsheimer). These powerful voices have inspired a great deal of debate in academic circles as well as in the public policy arena, and they will be put to good effect. Throughout the book, I will draw on this debate as I analyze specific country cases, consider policy dilemmas, and develop the three theses on globalization and state power that will anchor the concluding chapter. I hope that readers, in turn, will chart their own reactions to these strongly argued and quite contentious alternatives and use them as dramatic foils in reaching their own conclusions about the interactive effects of globalization and state power within a context of unrivaled American influence.

Part 1 introduces a set of in-depth comparative and regional studies of the effects of globalization on the capacities of states to secure desirable outcomes. The strength of the alternative perspectives will be tested against the specific dilemmas and challenges faced by a set of regionally diverse developed as well as developing countries.*

In Chapter 2, we begin with the United States and alternative interpretations of its standing as the hegemonic power. Do all states benefit from a global order shaped by American power and designed to sustain that power and advance American values? Or is American power exercised at the expense of other states? The chapter will confirm the unrivaled power and influence of the United States to control the geopolitical heights and shape global agendas in every dimension, revealing enormous competitive strengths as well as significant and perhaps surprising vulnerabilities. The chapter will argue that America is dominant but not omnipotent, and that the shift from America's tradition of strategic restraint to the Bush Doctrine's more muscular approach to the projection of American power is likely to prove both counter-productive and dangerously destabilizing.

Chapter 3 will discuss European traditions of social protection and social democracy, comparing British, German, and French economic and social models as a way of coming to terms with the underlying "clash of civilizations" that divides Europe and America even more than the sharp differences exposed by the war in Iraq. Are national economic models possible? Can "social Europe"

---

*To help facilitate cross-national comparisons and track developments across the range of processes associated with globalization, the book will include "Global Profiles" of a set of critical countries whose stories reveal particular insights about globalization and state power. The visual presentation of data will include key indicators of globalization in each of six dimensions: economic integration, information flows, people flows, political participation, cultural influences, and security and military interaction.

survive the strictures imposed by the economic and monetary integration pacts of the European Union? What are the geopolitical repercussions of the rancorous diplomatic divisions between key European powers and the United States? I will suggest that a careful analysis of the political prospects of key states within the prosperous and powerful regional bloc of the EU reveals that states possess a narrowing sphere of maneuver in this global era—and that the world's greatest experiment in multi-level governance may be creating more problems than it solves. No social and economic model is ruled out, but in each of our European cases governments face a tightening set of constraints on their exercise of power.

In Chapter 4, I extend the analysis to East Asia, scrutinizing the much-heralded "economic miracle" for what it tells us about alternative development models and government strategies to secure the benefits of a global economy. Does a comparison of alternative responses to the Asian financial crisis of 1997 reveal that different state strategies and capacities really matter—or that the movement of "hot money" can universally cause the melt down of local economies? What does a comparison of the exercise of state power in South Korea and Taiwan tell us about the range—and consequences—of alternative models for the exercise of state power? The chapter concludes with a timely discussion of U.S./China relations, a case that reveals with unusual clarity the economic vulnerabilities of the United States as well as the fascinating interplay between the politics of trade and the broader geopolitical agendas that structure relations between these two enormously powerful countries.

Finally, Part 2 considers key aspects of the transformation of global politics caused by 9/11. Against the backdrop of the war in Iraq and the resistance to occupation, Chapter 5 will analyze in detail the choices that have defined America's response to the terror attacks and evaluate the lessons of the war in Iraq for American geopolitical strategy and the prospects for reforming and revitalizing the United Nations. In Chapter 6, we will take up the implications of the new American empire for understanding the contemporary moment of globalization and conclude by presenting in detail our three theses on globalization, empire, and state power.

Before September 11, 2001, the economic aspects of globalization and the growing development gap were paramount. Since the attacks of September 11, 2001, concern about the "clash of civilizations" between the West and the Arab and Muslim world, the problem of security against terror, and questions about how American power will recast global alliances and affect both national politics and people's lives throughout the world, have partially refocused our thinking about globalization.

Taken together, the challenges of development and competitiveness, intensifying security threats, and the incessant demands for military and humanitarian intervention, have heightened the problems faced by government. As if that were not enough, this piling on of challenges is occurring in tandem with the unrelenting processes of globalization—from economic competition to multilevel governance—that compromise the ability of even the most powerful states to satisfy insecure and restive constituencies.

Hence, we are challenged as never before to develop a more complex understanding of globalization and how it shapes the behavior and the capacity of states throughout the world. I wrote the book in the hope that it will provide readers with the conceptual tools and the specific factual knowledge to achieve new understandings about some of the most critical political questions of our era—and then use those insights to engage in the policy debates that are driving politics and mobilizing citizens in nations across the globe.

ACKNOWLEDGMENTS

This book is in many ways a Wellesley book. It is a testament to the intellectual curiosity and global perspectives of the many Wellesley students who have taken my course "Globalization and the Nation-State" since it was introduced in spring 2000. Little did they know they were serving as a focus group for the arguments in this book, but I am immensely grateful for their assistance and the inspiration they provided. I am also enormously indebted to Anna Azaryeva for her exceptional work as a research assistant on this and related projects. In particular, I wish to thank Anna for her indefatigable efforts to overcome every quirk of data collection to assemble the Global Profiles and all the tables and figures that appear throughout the book. I would also like to thank Wellesley College for two Faculty Awards grants that supported the project and to express my gratitude to Norma Wilentz Hess for the ongoing generosity associated with my chair.

I extend my thanks to those who reviewed this book in its various manuscript stages and offered insightful feedback: Marc Belanger, Saint Mary's College; Cheryl L. Brown, University of North Carolina, Charlotte; Nigel Gibson, Emerson College; Heather Hindman, Denison University; Marvin S. Soroos, North Carolina State University; Linda Bishai, Towson University; Christopher L. Ball, Iowa State University.

I am indebted to David Coates for his encouragement and advice and, above all, for the pleasure of our ongoing collaborations, the benefits of which are evident here in both small and large ways. Of all the many friends and colleagues whose encouragement buoyed my efforts, I would especially like to thank Susie Albert, Anne Gillespie, Kelly Douglas, and Rebecca Figueroa.

I am very grateful to Eric Stano at Longman for his enthusiastic support and astute editorial advice. Thanks are also do to the project manager, Jared Sterzer, who was unfailingly professional and helpful throughout the production phase.

Finally, the greatest thanks, as always, go to those nearest and dearest, to my wife Carol, who understands as well as anyone the satisfactions and tribulations of writing books, and to our children, Nathan and Megan, who for the first time seemed to recognize what was involved. They provided an abundance of love and support, as well as a host of delightful alternatives to work, which made everything possible and a lot more fun.

CHAPTER I

Introduction: Globalization and the Challenges of Multi-level Governance

Consider the following scenes, each illustrating—like the loose pieces of colored glass in the rotating tube of a kaleidoscope—the continually shifting and endlessly captivating patterns of local and global interactions that comprise politics in the global era. They also disclose some key understandings about our core themes: how globalization complicates and often limits state power and how American power tends to distort and restrict the exercise of power by other states.

GLOBAL CONNECTIONS

Walking Your Dog: The Ghanaian Connection

If you are found dumping trash in Central Park or letting your dog foul a soft ball field in Queens—or caught in any of a thousand ways violating New York City's Department of Environmental Protection regulations—the hastily scrawled ticket thrust into your hand is likely to be processed in Ghana. On a three-shift cycle, 24 hours a day, in a nondescript office in Accra that is home to the busiest Internet center in West Africa, about 40 employees under contract to a data management firm based in Delaware work busily at their computer stations. They get three times the Ghanaian minimum wage to decipher the handwriting on the tickets, search a data base to locate the offender's name, address, the location of the infraction, and the fine, then type in the data and send it back to the United States within 48 hours of the offense.

As a *New York Times* reporter, Robert Worth put it, "through the alchemy of globalization, the tickets that bring only aggravation on this side of the Atlantic become snapshots that fire imaginations more than 5,000 miles away."[1] Viewing New York through the prism of environmental violations, the Ghanaians see the tumultuous "city that never sleeps" as an orderly haven. They imagine beautiful streets and beautiful people—why else would New Yorkers be so concerned about people's carelessness in cleaning up after their dogs? One of the data management employees said she could see herself living in New York, since she already knew the rules and regulations so well.

It seems that the data management company is a little less sanguine about the whole arrangement. Worried that the press reports might create some resentment among New Yorkers that a two-year city contract worth over $900,000 was taking jobs away from American workers, the firm is planning to expand its work in Ghana—but shift the data processing on its New York environmental protection account back to the United States. But there is nothing new—and nothing much likely to change—about the global outsourcing of data entry and the digitizing of information. Before the Delaware-based firm and the contract work in Ghana, the same work was done for a company based in Michigan by workers in Mexico and India.

The Taj Mahal in Texas?

Have you noticed the designer rice in your local whole foods or specialty shop, the one with the distinctive canister, the colorful label, and the name meant to evoke the famous aromatic basmati rice of South Asia? RiceTec, a corporation headquartered in Alvin Texas, markets products such as Jasmati, Kasmati, and Texmati to over 20,000 supermarkets in North America under the trademark RiceSelect. It has also been at the center of a huge controversy in the trade and patent wars that have been endemic to this era of globalization.

It all began in September 1997 when the U.S. Patent and Trademarks Office (USPTO) granted a series of patents to RiceTec for a cross-breed of American long-grain rice, granting it control over basmati rice production in North America and the right to collect fees from farmers who plant it. Round one of the controversy pitted the Indian government, rice growers and farmers, and global development and antipoverty activists against the U.S. Patents and Trademarks Office. India insisted that the name "basmati" should be applied only to the rice grown in the basmati region of India, claiming a similar status as Cognac or Champagne, and warning that Indian farmers and exporters faced a significant challenge to their lucrative international trade.

Behind the scientific and commercial issues were powerful cultural and nationalist appeals. "The Indian government also provided 50,000 pages of scientific argument to the Patents office, insisting that traditionally grown basmati rice already possessed the qualities claimed for the RiceTec variety to justify patent protection. You cannot build a monument anywhere and call it the Taj Mahal," argued the executive director of the All India Rice Exporters Association. "There is only one Taj Mahal and that is in India."[2]

As a result of India's scientific representations, backed by international pressure from citizens groups directed at the USPTO, the scope of the patents granted RiceTec was substantially narrowed in 2001. Then came round two, not yet fought to a conclusion. In June 2002 the European Union (EU) through the office of its Trade Commissioner launched an initiative at the Trade-Related Intellectual Property Rights (TRIPs) Council of the World Trade Organization (WTO) meeting in Geneva to protect traditional, high-quality products that are specific to particular regions—whether Parmigiano Reggiano, Limoges porcelain, or basmati rice. The United States through the U.S. Trade Representative, Robert B. Zoellick, promptly opposed the EU initiative. Zoellick argued that the system the EU offered—the establishment of a multilateral register of geographically based high-quality products— would "impose significant new costs on WTO members, especially developing and least developed members, which will far outweigh any potential benefits."[3]

Korea Stirred, Foreign Policy Shaken by James Bond?

North Korea throws out nuclear weapons inspectors from the International Atomic Energy Agency, pulls out of the Nuclear Nonproliferation Treaty (NPT), and threatens to restart weapons production and missile tests. Lights, camera, action. MGM releases a new James Bond thriller in South Korea on New Year's Eve 2003, amidst a dangerous (and continuing) show down between North Korea and the United States over the latter's nuclear weapon's program.

Could Hollywood's timing and taste be any worse? "James Bond appears to be achieving what years of political and military brinkmanship have failed to do—unite North and South Korea in a common cause," observed the British newspaper, *The Guardian*. "The makers of the twentieth 007 film, *Die Another Day,* have come under fire over their portrayal of North Korea as an evil regime hell-bent on world domination."[4] In the film, shot in Hawaii, Spain, Iceland, and Finland, Bond teams up with South Korean agents to thwart a scheme by a crazed North Korean commander to divide the two countries, literally, with a satellite laser and then invade Japan. The official news agency in the North decries the film's far-fetched depiction of the country as an "axis of evil"—the term coined by President George W. Bush in his 2002 State of the Union address—and a war-mongering effort to fan divisions between the two Koreas and mock the Korean nation.

Amidst a host of boycotts and demands that distribution of the film be halted, the reactions in South Korea include a local actor's refusal to accept an otherwise coveted bad-guy role in the film because of what he characterized as a "demeaning" script. Ten of the fifty theatres in Seoul pulled the film early, and passions ran so high that some protestors in the South praised North Korea's exit from the nonproliferation treaty announced in mid-January 2003. One South Korean activist called the timing of the release of the film "rather dangerous and not appropriate," as the film inspired grassroots denunciation of the United States and calls for Korean unification. The film spawned widespread and often passionate criticism on several grounds from the use of a Buddhist temple as the setting for one of Bond's sexual exploits to a scene in which an American military officer orders a South Korean mobilization to the final scene that depicts South Korean farmers with oxcarts.

Beyond the intriguing images and snapshot realities about the scale, scope, and variety of cross-border interactions that characterize globalization, these vignettes help expose the core themes at the heart of our investigation. In the instantaneous and seemingly random collisions between the local and the global, these "global moments" open a window into problems that all states face in controlling outcomes as well as America's unique capacity as hegemonic power to set agendas and block or reduce the exercise of state power by others.

Although too much should not be made of this rather light-hearted illustration of the workings of the global economy, the case of Ghanaian data entry clerks illustrates clearly one important truth: firms that can make the most of information technologies can "cherry-pick" employees anywhere who have the requisite skills and make them beneficiaries of a global economy. So far so good, but what are the political repercussions? Although we cannot be sure, it seems likely that the imagined orderliness of life in the Big Apple and the pull of higher wage rates may create an impetus for migration among a sizeable stratum of well trained and highly disciplined Ghanaians and perhaps foster a weakening of attachments to home. In addition, we can say with considerable certainty that the outsourcing of jobs from the United States has become a very volatile political issue with implications for the control of Congress and the White House. Outsourcing also plays a significant role in trade disputes that have bedeviled the United States in recent years, complicating its relations with allies and key trading partners, and absorbing a lot of the agenda of the WTO.

Meanwhile, Hollywood's demeaning and rather bellicose stereotypes of Koreans inspire anti-American sentiment and national unity on the Korean peninsula at a time of heightened regional tension and conflict between North Korea and the United States. By all appearances, it will be extremely difficult to persuade the North to give up its nuclear weapons program, particularly in a context that invites comparisons with Iraq. For North Korean leader Kim Jong Il the comparative lesson may well be that nuclear weapons are more important than ever as a deterrent against the United States.[5] In a context of complex regional diplomacy spurred by the United States, North Korean brinkmanship, and rising tensions, a film that galvanizes anti-American sentiment across the demilitarized zone makes little difference. But it is probably not what the state department—or the White House—had in mind! The movie certainly doesn't make American foreign policy in a nuclear showdown any easier and is a potent reminder that even the most powerful state in the world can't out-spin MGM or control every policy input.

The conflict over rice invites critical scrutiny of the capacity of developing states to advance sustainable development and protect powerful local interests in the face of global competitive pressures, harnessed by cutting-edge bio-technologies, and a policy regime backed by the United States. Indeed, the European Union versus United States battle over rice patents, TRIPs, and protection of local commodities that are especially prized in both economic and cultural terms opens a revealing window into the crucial theme of the linkage between our two core questions: does America's exercise of dominant power reduce the capacities of all other states to achieve their desired policy aims?

What significance should be attached to the fact that the United States and Europe are so often at loggerheads over trade issues? Do these disputes reflect nothing more than the natural competition of national and regional interests— or are they but the tip of the iceberg of differences in values, political cultures, and divergent perspectives about the responsibilities that the developed world have for the developing world? Perhaps there is even more at issue—a battle by the United States to control global agendas at the expense of its most powerful allies, an assertion of hegemony in the belief that state power is a zero sum game. Looked at for insights about the institutions of global governance, the various US/EU wars at the World Trade Organization tell us a great deal about the role and function of powerful international organizations, how they reflect and crystallize interstate rivalries and often bend to the will of the United States.

Taken together, these vignettes hint at the epochal changes driven by the sheer force of globalization and the far-reaching political consequences that leave no state untouched or untroubled. But an understanding of the full extent—and range—of globalization's influence on state power requires a broader perspective. Hence we move from anecdotal to more comprehensive evidence as we try to see the contours of globalization as a whole.

GLOBALIZATION: SEEING THE WHOLE ELEPHANT

Globalization includes the increasing spread of economic activities, seen in the reorganization of production and the global redistribution of the workforce (the "global factory") and in the increased extent and intensity of international trade, finance, and foreign direct investment. (See Figure 1.1 "World Foreign Direct Investment").

In addition, globalization involves the movement of peoples due to migration, employment, business, and educational opportunities. Globalization also involves the forging of new institutions of global governance, from the European Union to the World Trade Organization and the United Nations, all of which are

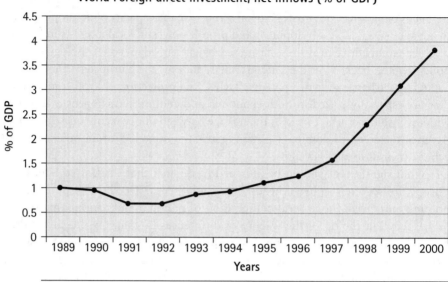

FIGURE 1.1

World Foreign direct investment, net inflows (% of GDP)

—•— Foreign direct investment, net inflows (% of GDP)

growing in both membership and influence. (See Figure 1.2 "Members of the United Nations").

Then there is the globalization of culture and style and the omnipresent corporate branding that penetrates everyday life such as the ubiquitous Sony Walkman, an icon at once of Japanese production and slick English language marketing, the prized possession of urban nomads from Detroit to Dar es Salaam, until MP3 players or the latest iPod (which has now overtaken computer sales in Apple's earnings profile[6]) came on the scene. Globalization involves a new transnational reach for legal regimes that has forced Pinochet, like a beleaguered Mafia boss, to plead age and infirmity to keep out of the dock and has put an unrepentant Milošević behind bars.

Finally, globalization includes other profound changes that are less visible but equally significant. For example, new applications of information technology (such as the Internet) distort the traditional distinction between what is around the world and what is around the block, thereby instantly transforming cultures, and blurring the boundaries between the local and global. Perhaps nothing captures the everyday experience of globalization more effectively than the exponential rise in Internet use in recent years. (See Figure 1.3 "Internet Users in the World"). At the same time, little captures the uneven access to globalization more vividly than Internet use that varies from over two-thirds of the population in North America to under 2 percent in Africa.

FIGURE 1.2
Members of the United Nations

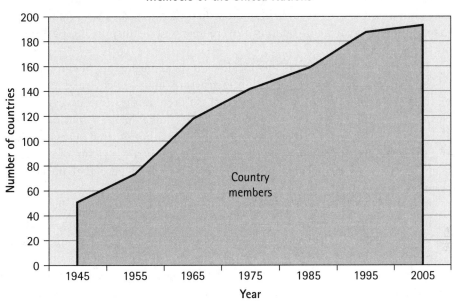

FIGURE 1.3
Internet Users in the World

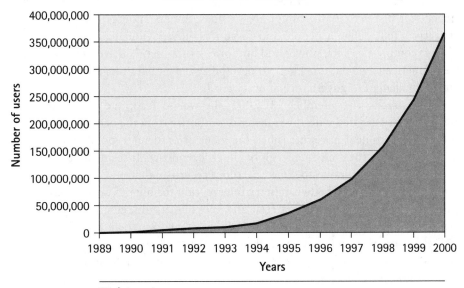

These technologies that make instantaneous communication possible link producers and contractors, headquarters, branch plants, and suppliers in "real time" anywhere in the world. Within the global economy, time is stretched out of shape, distance creates no friction to overcome, and distinctions in location are not as significant.

In the era of globalization, any locale with the requisite mix of entrepreneurial capabilities, education, technical infrastructure, and skill can take its rightful place in the global economy. Of course, these prerequisites for success tend to cluster, as they have for a very long time, in a familiar pattern that carves the globe into "haves" and "have-nots." But the stretching of time across space—and the sense that today's high-flying economy is tomorrow's victim of the Asian financial crisis—is significant enough to send a chill of perpetual uncertainty across the globe.

Recalling our three-part definition of globalization, viewed broadly through a panoramic lens, these processes describe the scope of globalization: the growing depth, extent, and diversity of cross-border connections that are a signal characteristic of the contemporary world. The uneven distribution of opportunities in an invidious North/South pattern speaks to the contradictory character of globalization and the inherent divisiveness of globalization noted in the second part of our definition.

Above all, in accordance with the third component of our definition, we wish to emphasize the political consequences of globalization. All these processes complicate politics as they erode the ability of even the strongest nation-states to control their destinies. No states can secure economic and life cycle security for their citizens. None can preserve pristine "national models" of economic governance—or distinctly national cultures, values, understandings of the world, or narratives that define a people and forge their unity. Globalization is unavoidable; it compromises the power and authority of states and, driven by a muscular new American agenda, it is likely to destabilize the global order and present profound challenges to governance at every level.

The attacks of September 11, 2001, the war in Iraq, and the conflict and uncertainty associated with the transfer of authority from the occupying forces to an Iraqi government have intensified the focus of academics, policy-makers, and citizens alike on the dark side of global interdependence. It seems that everyone's attention has been drawn to concerns about security, what new rules and norms will govern war, and whether military intervention for humanitarian ends is even possible in a context where material and geopolitical interests hold sway. How will unrivaled American power recast global alliances, redefine the agendas of global governance, and affect both the capacities of states to secure desirable outcomes and the capacity of citizens throughout the world to lead the lives to which they aspire?

More than ever globalization, as revised by the new challenges of the post-9/11 world, frames the way politics is experienced and the way it is studied. In turn, applying the global lens to political analysis will inevitably put new interpretations of the role, function, durability, and coherence of nation-states into clearer focus.

HISTORIC CHALLENGES TO STATE AND NATION

Globalization may be the greatest historic transformation since the Industrial Revolution, with similarly paradoxical effects on the lived experience of the generations that feel the full brunt of the contemporary upheaval. Historian E. P. Thompson captures this point unmistakably for the Industrial Revolution:

Over the period 1790–1840 there was a slight improvement in average material standards. Over the same period there was intensified exploitation, greater insecurity, and increasing human misery. By 1840 people were "better off" than their forerunners had been fifty years before, but they had suffered and continue to suffer this slight improvement as a catastrophic experience.[7]

Will we in hindsight come to experience globalization similarly, as an historic upheaval that increases insecurity even for the better off and overlays success with a patina of catastrophe?

I think it is fair to say that globalization contributes to a pervasive, chronic uncertainty about the future at every level of society everywhere, although by no means equally. Can I keep my job (or can my business compete)? Will my children have the education and competitive skills they need? What does it mean these days to be an American or (fill in the blank with your own nationality)? Will I be secure in my old age? What cultural and moral values can reasonably be preserved in the face of international competitiveness and the deeply held convictions of others?

Particularly in the period since September 11, 2001, the fear of attacks from global terrorist networks, concerns for personal as well as national security, as well as unease in many quarters about the implications of a war against terror with no end in view, threaten to make a new visceral insecurity a permanent fixture in life—and a never-ending challenge to the nation-state. In this context, it is no exaggeration to observe that globalization fosters endemic insecurity in everyday life and presents extraordinary challenges to government.

For centuries "nation-states" have been the basic building blocks of politics. Nations are defined by "imagined communities,"[8] shared cultures and fates. Historically, *nations* have been politically organized and empowered by *states* that deliver the goods. States coordinate the economy, providing the institutions for governance and both social and military security. States have the capacity to represent people and groups and forge commonality. They consecrate the legal order and help inspire deep loyalties. When people die for their country, they are dying for nation and state, taken together. We are willing to risk everything to preserve everything that matters: a way of life that encompasses a sense of unique identity, an ethnic-national heritage, a set of values, a material quality of life, the pleasures of every day social interactions in family and community.

Although moral and cosmopolitan convictions can run very deep, few would die for the principles of the Universal Declaration of Human Rights. Nobody thus far has gone to the barricades shouting, "Long live the European Union!" The norm of the nation-state—or more simply put "a country"—provides clear boundaries for citizenship, the abiding sense of shared fates, and loyalties.

The depth of these attachments that bind communities of fate, affection, and identity seems nearly impossible without an essential attribute of the political community: boundedness. At its core, the notion of a nation-state involves a strong sense of territoriality. Thus, the dominion of the state is explicitly affirmed by border controls and more subliminally reinforced by the sense of national distinctiveness that draws a line between citizen and foreigner, domestic politics and international affairs, sovereignty within the borders and the anarchy of competing states outside the border without the benefit of the binding rule of law.

The one-to-one correspondence between a nation or people and the exclusive political organization of a given territory by a state has achieved almost theological force: it is treated as the only suitable way to divide the world into stable and respectable units. Yet, the frequency of this arrangement was always exaggerated. In fact, borders very rarely coincide with a single national group in the sense of a people with common ethnic ancestry ("blood ties") or even a people exhibiting the more amorphous feeling of belonging or sameness. Nation-states are very much the exception. Thirty-five years ago scholars thought that perhaps 10 percent or fewer states could properly be called nation-states.[9] Today, in this era of immigration and cultural diffusion, it is difficult to think of any pure cases of a culturally, linguistically, and ethnically homogeneous population (the nation) corresponding exactly to the territorial-juridical limits of sovereign control (the state).

The concept of the nation, as a distinct cultural unit, encased in a state protected from all intruders by bright line territorial boundaries seems increasingly suspect. Borders create little friction. Internet, telephone, and e-mail traffic pass unimpeded. Economic transactions performed by private actors are loosely regulated. All kinds of cultural media enter our homes and consciousness wherever we may live, and travelers from refugees to business executives find their way across, whether through bleak frontiers or posh airport lounges. All these cross-border processes associated with globalization chip away at the core territoriality of the state and erode the distinctiveness of national cultures.

It is clear that the nation-state faces a host of challenges simultaneously from above and below. The capacities of states to achieve desirable domestic policy outcomes without assistance or negotiation and assert effective control over their sovereign territories are compromised by regional and global technological and market forces, as well as growing security concerns. Ethnic, nationalist, and religious divisions that often involve both local and external components simultaneously assault their very stability and viability. Indeed the very definitions of the nation-state, nationalism, and citizenship are changing under pressures such as the emergence of global cities as transnational centers that have little connection to their surroundings[10] and escalating worldwide immigration.

The consequences of globalization for the nation—as distinct from the state—receive relatively little attention. Yet, it is plain that globalization erodes both sides of the equation. Cross-cultural influences, transnational identities, and the colonial, post-colonial, and post-Cold War displacements of nations and the redesign of states have transformed this most basic of all political units. It is not uncommon for peoples and nations to be perpetually in search of states of their own or for states to be under assault by the multiple nations they encompass. In the face of the multiethnic, multireligious, immigrant realities of nearly all countries, the cultural glue of the nation is losing its adhesive quality. Citizenship, loyalty, and a sense of shared fates are stretched. The attachments of citizens are weakened or spread across several levels of governance.

FROM AUTONOMY TO MULTI-LEVEL GOVERNANCE

For centuries, the political role of nation-states (countries) was framed by a taken-for-granted assumption of *sovereignty,* understood as exclusive authority over domestic and foreign affairs. A country's domestic politics was nestled within an interstate system that has been called the *Westphalian model* (referring to the Peace of Westphalia of 1648, which ended the German phase of the Thirty Years War). The model assumes a world of autonomous sovereign states, operating by national interest, with diplomatic relations and recourse to force, but with minimal cooperation.[11] Above all, the Westphalian model asserts two principles—territoriality and autonomy, defined by the exclusion of external actors from exercising authority or effective control within the borders of a given state.[12]

The norm of nonintervention in domestic affairs meant that borders were sacrosanct. Hence rulers were always at liberty to determine domestic political arrangements without external interference. According to this increasingly anachronistic model of insular and autonomous states, interference in domestic affairs was by invitation only. All members of the European Union, for example, were free to accept (as they have) that rulings of the European Court of Justice were binding and those that join the euro club might likewise accept the transfer of control over monetary policy to the external authority of the European Central Bank. Likewise participation in international organizations such as the United Nations or NATO—or acceptance of the economic policies imposed on governments by the International Monetary Fund and the World Bank as the condition for receiving much-needed loans—could be said to represent the voluntary modification of the noninterference principle.

Some have sought to accommodate these cases within the classic principles of the Westphalian model of sovereignty, but it would be a stretch to interpret structural adjustment programs as an exercise of free choice. When it comes to the European Union, it would seem to take a death-defying leap into the void to ignore the transformation of the principle of sovereignty that has been rendered. Surely, we cannot overlook the historic importance of an intergovernmental system that is anchored in pooled sovereignty, firmly established in treaties, codified by a formal constitutional document (provisionally approved in June 2004) that will govern the political behavior of 25 countries if and when ratification is achieved.

Many observers would agree that there is an inherent—and growing tension—between sovereignty defined by bounded territorial authority and globalization understood as a growing intensification and multiplicity of cross-border processes and influences beginning with the globalization of economic activities. Saskia Sassen captures this development well:

> *Economic globalization represents a major transformation, not only in the territorial organization of economic activity, but also in the organization of political power, notably sovereignty as we have known it. Today the major dynamics at work in the global community have the capacity to undo the intersection of sovereignty and territory embedded in the modern state and the modern inter-state system.*[13]

The "unbundling of sovereignty," as Sassen calls this historic rupture between territorial control and sovereignty, makes great demands on the state to function differently if it is to function effectively in a radically changed environment, one in which it cannot operate as autonomously and authoritatively as before.

Today, it seems that no states can defend their territory against terror attacks, the cross-border mobility of information as well as capital, the influence of multinational corporations or transnational social movements, and the value-forming and cultural influences of Mickey Mouse and McDonald's,[14] not to mention James Bond in the two Koreas or the images of America conveyed to the data-entry clerks in Accra by the tickets they are processing. It appears that we are entering a new era of politics in which it is anachronistic and potentially misleading to presuppose a political baseline of exclusive territorial control. States face an historic challenge: to reassert the integrative and consensus building of the polity within a context framed by nonexclusive authority and brokered sovereignty. That is why much of the debate about globalization has focused on its corrosive effects on the capacities and sovereignty of the state.

A set of international regimes (trade, environment, legal), global markets, and regional trading blocs (above all, the European Union) all compromise the sovereignty of the state. No state or international governmental or nongovernmental organization, even the most powerful, can secure desirable outcomes autonomously. Thus multi-level governance is the characteristic framework for politics today. Even more than the intensification of world trade or investment, this emerging framework of overlapping, incomplete, and competing sovereignties captures the defining feature of the contemporary global age. It provides the lens for making sense of globalization and state power.

Multi-level governance is here to stay, and not only in Europe. It has become increasingly common in academic as well as policy circles to discuss the *unraveling* of the central state and the reallocation and dispersal of decision-making authority in various directions: upwards (to the supranational level), downwards (to the sub-national region or local government), and sideways (through functional and overlapping jurisdictions to provide specific services with the greatest efficiency). There is a huge political science, federalism, and international relations literature analyzing the record of how the centralized authority of the nation-state has become increasingly dispersed, what menu of institutional options concerning governance has emerged, and how to access the virtues and vices of different models of multi-level governance.[15]

It is a fundamental maxim guiding the analysis here that the growing extent, frequency, and entrenchment of cross-border processes—what we mean by globalization—have changed the equation when it comes to the exercise of state power. Westphalian sovereignty is gone, never to be seen again. Increasingly, states are bound up in complex institutionalized interdependencies, some more voluntary then others, and some sufficiently institutionalized to constitute multi-level governance. Some of these arrangements, in turn, have become sufficiently entrenched that it will be difficult or impossible for most states to exert effective independent decision-making in critical policy domains from economic governance to national security. Adding to the challenges that states are now facing, we must include the challenge posed by the dominance of the United States in economic, military, and geopolitical spheres and the assertive global strategies pursued in accordance with the post-9/11 projection of power heralded by the Bush doctrine. This theme will be developed in detail in Chapter 2.

Some observers have claimed that globalization has hastened the declining authority of the state, suggesting "the heads of government may be the last to recognise that they and their ministers have lost the authority over national societies and economies they used to have."[16] Others have gone further, anouncing the demise of the nation-state. Consider, for example, Kenichi Ohmae, the most influential advocate of the claim that radical mobility of factors of production has effectively swamped the capacities of the nation-state. Ohmae argues that the transition to a "borderless economy" spurred by the diffusion of information technologies explodes the conventional view that nation-states are the basic unit of economic activity and the institutional setting for advancing alternative models and strategies.[17]

The argument here starts from very different assumptions. At the heart of this book is the conviction that states matter: globalization has not erased that fundamental truth about the world of politics, although it has refined it. We have described the power of the international system—whether that power is expressed in economic, geopolitical or military terms—to transform and constrain the exercise of state power. But as Peter Gourevitch has argued with great clarity, although the international system shapes domestic politics, there are always alternatives. Domestic politics—institutional arrangements, ideological preferences, and partisan considerations—determine what choices are made.[18]

At the same time, as we shall see in the analysis that follows, the most powerful states, and particularly the United States, can exert enormous influence in the way they shape the institutions of economic and global governance—from the World Trade Organization to the United Nations—to serve their national interests and advance their geopolitical agendas. In the end, as Alexander Wendt observed, "States still are at the center of the international system, and as such it makes no more sense to criticize a theory of international politics as 'state-centric' than it does to criticize a theory of forests for being 'tree-centric.'"[19] To that extent, our analysis is state-centric, even if globalization and multi-level governance (not to mention the powerful pull exerted by U.S. hegemony) have left the trees shaken root and branch.

GLOBALIZATION AND STATE POWER:
PARADIGMS LOST

The revolutions of 1989 in Eastern and Central Europe marked the demise of much of the communist world. When the Berlin Wall, which divided East and West, was pulled down brick by brick in November 1989, the architecture of Europe—and with it the world political order—was transformed. Within a year Germany was unified. By the end of 1991, the Soviet Union had splintered into fifteen wary and troubled republics. For better or worse, the geopolitical order lost its grim predictability and, with the demise of the Cold War, the consensus about a conceptual framework and terminology for defining the era evaporated.

The search is on for a new paradigm that will capture the logic of today's international order as vividly and comprehensively as the term Cold War did for the period from the end of World War II to the start of the 1990s. In many ways, the debates about globalization and state power have become the terrain on which these architectonic battles for defining the contemporary global era are fought. From this huge literature, we select four interlocutors—Thomas Friedman, Samuel Huntington, Joseph Stiglitz, and John Mearsheimer—to frame the debate and analysis in the pages that follow. Each controversial in his own way, all erudite and influential, their work spans a range of theoretical and ideological perspectives and helps crystallize some key understandings that have emerged from the unusually contentious dispute about globalization and state power.

The Golden Straightjacket

Thomas Friedman of the *New York Times* says simply that the "globalization system" has replaced the Cold War system. For Friedman, globalization, defined as an inexorable integration of markets, is the "overarching international system" that shapes both domestic politics and foreign relations. If the Berlin Wall was the symbol of Cold War division, then the World Wide Web is the unifying symbol of globalization.

In principle, wrote Friedman in *The Lexus and the Olive Tree,* the defining challenge of this era for individuals as for countries is to "find a healthy balance between preserving a sense of identity, home and community and doing what it takes to survive within the globalization system."[20] In practice, the pressures of imperious free-market capitalism (the Lexus) are paramount. The policies needed to establish market confidence in any government or national economy (such as balanced budgets, privatization, relatively low taxes, and minimal government regulation of markets) comprise a "Golden Straightjacket." Put it on and your economy grows while your politics shrinks. Your country's political choices are reduced to Pepsi or Coke. Take it off, and your government and country face certain disaster.

Friedman's is an era where footloose capital—depicted as the "Electronic Herds" of millions of investors moving vast sums of money instantly around the world at mouse click speed—can trample currencies, trading blocs, and governments in a matter of days. Enduring local cultures and values and traditions have their appeal, but Lexus trumps olive tree every time. As a result, the only culture that matters is the largely American culture of Mickey Mouse, iMacs and Big Macs. As an unfortunate byproduct, this culture of globalization generates a backlash against America among those who resent the rich and powerful, become too sentimental about local cultures, or get trampled for their iconoclasm.

Increasingly in his writing, particularly in his extended set of commentaries on the post-September 11 global order compiled in *Longitudes and Attitudes*[21], Friedman has shifted his emphasis away from the tension between local cultures and the processes of globalization. Instead, as he attempted to "fully comprehend who the nineteen suicide hijackers who burst into our lives on 9/11 were, and what motivated them to do what they did, and what motivated large arts of the Arab and Muslim worlds to give them passive support,"[22] a theme that was a minor chord in *The Lexus and the Olive Tree* emerged with greater clarity. Globalization, modernization, and democratization can bridge the gap between the Lexus and the olive tree.

In his earlier work, Friedman suggested that the sense of family and nation (olive trees) ground us. They "provide the feelings of self-esteem and belonging that are as essential for human survival as food in the belly."[23] After 9/11, he made a subtle but important shift. Dignity required jobs and opportunities and freedom of expression, the public goods that only democracy and globalization could provide—at the expense of local cultures of authoritarian leadership and preoccupation with the "old agenda of the Arab-Israeli conflict."[24] *Longitudes and Attitudes* may be read as an impassioned exhortation to young middle-class Arabs and Muslims and progressive leaders (Friedman nominates Jordan's King Abdullah) to transform the culture and political sensibility of the Middle East and enjoy the full benefits of globalization as well as the peace and security that would go with it.

A second incremental shift came with the war in Iraq. The war inspired a series of commentaries that mixed skepticism about the justifications given for the war—such as the linkage between Al-Qaeda and Saddam Hussein or how imminent the threat of weapons of mass destruction (WMD) really was—with passionate support for the invasion, nonetheless. "Sometimes smashing someone in the face is necessary to signal others that they will be held accountable for the intolerance they incubate," wrote Friedman. "Removing the Taliban and Saddam sent the message to every government in the area. . . . [T]he war may have created more hatred for the U.S., but it has also triggered a hugely important dialogue among Arabs and Muslims about the necessity of reform."[25] In this sense, the war in Iraq placed on the agenda new prospects for the democratic reform of states.

Friedman's argument here provides critical support for the third thesis on globalization and state power (globalization as the engine of democracy and progress), which will be revisited in Chapter 6.

The Clash of Civilizations

For Harvard University's Samuel Huntington in *The Clash of Civilizations and the Remaking of World Order,* the years since the end of the Cold War have witnessed a fundamental paradigm shift of a very different sort than Friedman describes, with none of the transformative potential for the Muslim and Arab world. During the Cold War, ideological differences and superpower politics defined the global order. Today global politics has been reconfigured along cultural lines. "For peoples seeking identity and reinventing ethnicity, enemies are essential," writes Huntington, "and the potentially most dangerous enmities occur across the fault lines between the world's major civilizations."[26]

In Huntington's analysis, civilizations are the broadest cultural unit at the apex of villages, regions, ethnic groups, nationalities, and religious groups. They are huge agglomerations: the world is divided into but seven or eight major civilizations. Deep-seated cultural differences, and not Friedman's technologically driven market forces, are the root causes of today's fundamental disparities in political and economic development. Muslim culture largely determines the failure of democracy in much of the Islamic world, while the West is the culture of modernization, industrialization, innovation, and the "American Creed."

The key issues and conflicts on the horizon of world politics involve differences or clashes between civilizations. The central axis of conflict has shifted from U.S./Soviet rivalry to the clash of Western and non-Western civilizations, particularly Islam. It is thus a two-front war, defined first by a fault line that has migrated several hundred miles east of the Iron Curtain. The central divide is defined by a line running though the former Soviet Union and Yugoslavia as well as through the Ukraine, Sudan, Nigeria, and many other countries. This line divides the peoples of Western Christianity from the Muslim and Orthodox peoples. A second front is homeland defense: the clash in America between defenders of Western civilization and multiculturalists. As Huntington puts it starkly, "The futures of the United States and the West depend upon Americans reaffirming their commitment to Western civilization."[27]

In our analysis, Huntington's argument, with a different twist, will be discussed in Chapter 3, as we come to terms with the clash of civilizations within Europe between Christian and Muslim peoples. In addition, Huntington's contention that Western intervention creates an impetus for democratization and modernization provides an important element of the third thesis on globalization and state power (globalization as the engine of democracy and progress) to which we will return in Chapter 6.

Both Friedman and Huntington have animated the debate about the current global order of politics with clear, provocative, and insightful arguments. No one who witnessed Asia tumble into a banking and financial crisis in 1997 could doubt the potency of Friedman's electronic herds or the consequences that follow when the Golden Straightjacket is no longer seen to fit. And since September 11, a great many people—not least among them senior American policymakers—have been hard pressed to resist the almost hypnotic appeal of Huntington's clash of civilizations paradigm.

Paradoxically, these two "big-picture" interpretations of the contemporary global order tend to cancel each other out. Friedman's world is a strangely futuristic apparition: a world with no civilizations where tribe and ethnicity provide very little friction. It is a world animated by global markets and the lure of information technologies, where a culture of footloose capital and pressures of perpetual innovation cross every border and swamp all local cultures and political alternatives. One set of policies fits all. By contrast, in Huntington's vision, cultural legacies from the distant past hold the future hostage. As Friedman observes, "For Huntington, only tribalism could follow the Cold War, not anything new."[28] Despite these important differences in perspective, Friedman and Huntington converge in their affirmation of the globalization as the engine of democracy thesis.

Of course, both these books have their share of enthusiasts as well as detractors, and they have generated extensive commentaries that raise questions about method, historical accuracy, and validity of interpretive frameworks. In a multi-sided debate about the defining principles and emerging trajectories of the global political order, these contributions are almost as important for what they leave out: fine-grained, conceptually rigorous accounts of the role of states. To understand how globalization shapes political developments, we need to apply more focused attention to the role of states—as the players that pull the strings of dominant international organizations and as competitors for power in the international system.

Broken Promises

To be sure, there are different ways to bring the state back in. We have Joseph P. Stiglitz, a Nobel Prize winning economist, who has also served as the chairman of the Council of Economic Advisers and chief economist of the World Bank, to thank for one of the most critical and influential interpretations of the role of states in the era of globalization. With his background, it is no surprise that Stiglitz associates globalization with the closer integration of countries and peoples driven first and foremost by the intensification of cross-border economic transactions made possible by "an enormous reduction of costs of transportation and communication, and the breaking down of artificial barriers to the flow of goods, services, capital, and knowledge, and (to a lesser extent) people across borders."[29] Offering a distinctive definition of globalization, Stiglitz also emphasizes the new institutions that govern globalization, such as the World Bank, the World Trade Organization (WTO), and especially the International Monetary Fund (IMF).

Even with Stiglitz's reputation as a reformer, the uncompromising vehemence of his critique of these institutions and the power brokers behind them is startling. "The critics of globalization accuse Western countries of hypocrisy," argues Stiglitz, "and they are right."[30] They pressure developing countries to tear down trade barriers, but protect their own industries from competition in agricultural products where developing countries might have the advantage. And even where they are not hypocritical, the West and the United States as the "prime culprit" exploit every opportunity to control the globalization agenda and advance their own interests.

Globalization and Its Discontents is a thorough analysis of how powerful states—and, in particular the key industrial countries that comprise the Group of 7[31]—have hijacked the institutions that govern globalization and steered the IMF away from its original mission. According to Stiglitz, although the IMF was founded "on the belief that markets often work badly, it now champions market supremacy with ideological fervor."[32] Founded on the belief that international pressure and support should encourage expansionary policies, like increasing government expenditures or lower interest rates to create jobs and stimulate the economy, the IMF now insists on policies such as reducing expenditures on education, health care, and infrastructure and increasing interest rates that lead to a contraction in the economy, increased misery and insecurity.

The "Washington Consensus"—the ideologically driven policy consensus of the IMF, the World Bank, and the U.S. Treasury, which looks quite a lot like Friedman's "Golden Straightjacket"—forces developing countries to open their borders to the unregulated trade competition and the "hot money" invited in (and just as quickly back out) by the rapid, premature liberalization (opening) of capital markets. "Small developing countries are like small boats," observes Stiglitz. "Rapid capital market liberalization, in the manner pushed through by the IMF, amounted to setting them off on a voyage on a bright sea, before the holes in their hulls have been repaired, before the captain has received training, before life vests have been put on board."[33]

Worst of all, the promise of the IMF to stabilize the global economy and eliminate poverty has been broken not because of errors of judgment but, according to Stiglitz, because of fundamental flaws in institutional design. The IMF, like its Washington Consensus partners, is dominated by the wealthiest countries. But who speaks for those countries? At the IMF, the seats around the table are reserved for the governors of central banks and finance ministers. So the G7 controls the IMF and the representatives of the G7 see the world through the lens of leading commercial and financial interests.

States matter, but some states matter more than others, and the power of the United States is usually decisive. By contrast, citizens are left on the outside looking in—or on the streets to mobilize their antiglobalization backlash. We will return to Stiglitz in Chapter 4 for his considerable insights on the Asian economic crisis. In addition, Stiglitz's argument that the United States enjoys a unique capacity to control financial markets and international trade both directly and by pulling the strings in key arenas of global governance helps substantiate the analysis of America's global economic and geopolitical dominance in Chapter 2. It also provides important support for Thesis 1 on globalization and state power (the invisible hand thesis), which emphasizes the manifold benefits that flow to the United States from the Washington Consensus and from the rules that govern the central pillars of global economic governance such as the IMF and the WTO.

Offensive Realism

In *The Tragedy of Great Power Politics*,[34] John Mearsheimer, a political scientist at the University of Chicago, observes that most of the great debates in international relations theory pit theorists across the great divide between realism and liberalism (or within those camps). Both traditions treat states as central actors, with realists emphasizing that the behavior of states is mainly shaped by their external environment, and liberals arguing that the internal characteristics of states (such as the distinction between democracies and dictatorships, "good" and "bad" states) shape their behavior. Liberals expect democracies to be more cooperative and less bellicose than dictatorships, view high levels of economic interdependence to be stabilizing, and contend that international institutions moderate behavior. According to the liberal paradigm, international institutions lead states to acquire new values and recognize the benefit of mutually supporting interests.[35] Realists, on the contrary, downplay the significance of internal differences among states in regime type, culture, ideology, or institutional arrangements. States inhabit a zero-sum world of competition over power, which is intense, dangerous, and unforgiving. Regardless of their form of government, all states are alike: they are like billiard balls, varying only in size and the force they might exert when striking others.

Globalization is not the concept that inspires Mearsheimer's understanding of the contemporary global order. In *The Tragedy of Great Power Politics,* the term "globalization" does not even appear in the index and reasonably enough, since Mearsheimer argues that the systemic properties of the international order are no different today than they were before. His core concept is the eternal verity of politics—power, which drives state behavior for all realists. "Power is the currency of great-power politics, and states compete for it among themselves," observes Mearsheimer. "What money is to economics, power is to international relations."[36]

Perhaps the most compelling and influential academic proponent of the realist approach for its value in understanding international relations systems and great power politics, Mearsheimer takes the paradigm to its logical conclusion. He challenges the status quo bias of structural realism (relabeled *defensive realism* by Mearsheimer), which emphasizes how in a state of anarchy the international system produces varying patterns of behavior of states, that have little to do with the intentions of states and far more to do with the characteristics of the global order. He agrees that in a world without authoritative institutions or effective norms, states rely on their own power to protect themselves and advance their interests. But Mearsheimer rejects defensive realism for supposing that anarchy makes states risk averse, discouraging states from pressing to gain power at the expense of others, and assuming a tendency toward a relatively stable balance-of-power equilibrium.

Mearsheimer's theory—which he calls *offensive realism*—is a structural theory as well, in which the behavior of states is shaped by the international system. However, it throws out the assumptions of defensive realism that just enough is good enough, and that there are few incentives to aggrandize power. He argues, on the contrary, that all states want—and should want—more power than they possess, and any who have the opportunity will grasp for the ring of hegemonic power, the capacity to dominate all other states in the international system.

Mearsheimer is admirably direct and transparent. Offensive realism is mainly a descriptive theory about how great powers have behaved in the past and how they are likely to behave at present and in the future. "But it is also a prescriptive theory," maintains Mearsheimer. "States *should* behave according to the dictates of offensive realism, because it outlines the best way to survive in a dangerous world."[37]

Mearsheimer may be right to say that Americans instinctively prefer the liberal paradigm because they are optimistic, high-minded about values, and want to think that democracy matters a great deal. Nevertheless, in this era of global politics defined in no small measure by the unrivaled military power of the United States and the application of a strategic doctrine of preemption (or as we will discuss in Chapter 5, "prevention") to match America's muscle, Mearsheimer is on everyone's "A list." He makes one of the most compelling—and certainly the most timely—cases for the antiglobalization skeptics who argue that we have seen all this before and globalization does not define a new era of international politics.

"Mearsheimer has spent over twenty years drawing widely upon historical case studies to buttress his contention that physical power—a combination of military effectiveness, economic strength, population size, and geographical extent—is the key to explaining what goes on in international politics, and understanding how events unfold the way they do," observed historian Paul Kennedy in a review of the *Tragedy of Great Power Politics*.[38] As Kennedy adds, for Mearsheimer no contemporary developments, whether the formation of the United Nations system or the processes of democratization and globalization have changed that elemental truth.

The force of Mearsheimer's clear-headed analysis of great power politics will be put to good use in the analysis that follows. In Chapter 2, his concept of defensive realism will help crystallize the strategic restraint that characterized the American geopolitical consolidation of the liberal world order after World War II. In addition, Mearsheimer's analysis that economic interdependence has not quelled the incessant struggle for power (often with hostile intent) that characterizes great power politics provides a crucial link, as we shall see in Chapter 4, between the financial crisis in East Asia and geopolitical and military insecurity in the region. Finally, as we discuss in Chapter 6, Mearsheimer's analytic framework offensive realism is extremely helpful in coming to terms with the new national security strategy of the United States and its application to the war in Iraq.

What can be learned from our virtual debate between Stiglitz and Mearsheimer, two advocates of a strong state model of the global order, with very different perspectives? Mearsheimer would no doubt view Stiglitz's radical reform agenda with considerable skepticism. He would reject the central importance Stiglitz assigns to international institutions of economic governance, and regard any reform agenda for the IMF, the World Bank, or the WTO that requires the G7 to accept reduced power as unrealistic at best. In rebuttal, Stiglitz would likely question Mearsheimer's claim that the structure of the international system is as anarchic as ever, and that international institutions are all but powerless to effect significant change.

In part, the disagreements between Stiglitz and Mearsheimer result from their different policy domains. In areas of economic policy institutionalized cooperation may look more robust than in military strategy. When Mearsheimer says, "there is no institution with any real power in Asia,"[39] he is probably thinking less about the role of the IMF in the Asian financial crisis of 1997, and more about the absence of a regional organization equivalent to NATO or the European Union that can perhaps force states to act against their perceived strategic goals. And, it is worth noting, Mearsheimer and Stiglitz agree that the most powerful states create, shape, and use institutions—not as altruistic concessions to check their own power on the world stage, but rather to maintain or increase it. Viewed that way, the role of the G7 in Stiglitz's institutions of economic governance may be seen to approximate Mearsheimer's doctrine of offensive realism. When these two powerful voices agree across their formidable divide, the rest of us should probably pay close attention.

Huntington and Friedman, Stiglitz and Mearsheimer, have very different views about the strength or weakness of states, the importance of democracy and democratic reforms, the persistence of cultures and civilizations, and the role of international institutions in shaping the behavior of states. We will return to these key contributors to the globalization debate many times in the pages ahead as different dimensions of state power and different processes of globalization come into focus. Taken together, these four worthy interlocutors reveal the intensity of the debate—and the raw intellectual power—that has been brought to bear on the core questions we address in this book. How has globalization reconstituted the role and function of states? How does the exercise of hegemonic power by the United States shape the global order, limit the power of competing states, and affect the contours of American politics?

These are urgently important questions and the answers matter a great deal. Disputes about globalization and state power inspire spellbinding intellectual debates and frame critical divides in national politics. They are also especially fertile ground for informed and reasoned reflection about the future course of American and global politics. Readers are invited to take sides and, at the same time, encouraged to take seriously each of the three theses on globalization and state power that drive the analysis, for they offer distinctive interpretations on the exercise of U.S. power and its consequences for the global order.

Thesis 1 (the invisible hand) contends that the unrivaled power of the United States is expressed first and foremost in the very architecture of the global economic system, which uniquely privileges the United States at the expense of every other state in the world. Thesis 2 (the contested sovereignty of the state) argues for the central importance of multi-level governance which, in combination with a broad array of transnational and international forces, reduces the capacity of all states—including the United States—to achieve its goals and control the external environment. America remains the unrivaled first among unequal states, but remains subject nonetheless to potential shifts in the inter-state balance of power and reversals of fortune. Thesis 3 (globalization as the engine of democracy) advances the view that globalization spurs the creation of an entrepreneurial middle class in countries throughout the world and with it the diffusion of a political order that is nourished by democratic values—and underwritten by American hegemony.

Each thesis provides coherent and potentially compelling answers to each of the questions that motivates this study. At another level, they offer alternative visions of the United States—and of global politics—that speak to deeply held beliefs and values. There is no morally neutral or politically impartial answer to the question: "Who wins when America rules?"

With the help of our interlocutors and with the powerful alternatives represented by the theses outlined above (to be developed more fully in Chapter 6), we begin our inquiry into state power in the global era by turning first to the most influential global player, the United States.

PART I

STATE POWER IN THE ERA OF GLOBALIZATION

CHAPTER II

Globalization and the Exercise
of American Power

The United States is undoubtedly the hegemonic power in the contemporary global order and has been for more than 50 years. It remains dominant today, despite the daunting challenges and transformed context wrought by the terror attacks of September 11, 2001. In fact, the United States is so dominant that it is easy to forget that both the duration and extent of its extraordinary—some say historically unique—preponderance of power in military, economic, and geopolitical terms was not always taken for granted. "Most observers have expected dramatic shifts in world politics after the Cold War such as the disappearance of American hegemony, the return of great power balancing, the rise of competing regional blocs, and the decay of multilateralism," observed G. John Ikenberry before 9/11, the "Bush revolution" in American foreign policy, and the war in Iraq. "Yet despite expectations of great transformations and new world orders, the half-century-old American order is still the dominant reality in world politics today."[1]

The war in Iraq has magnified concerns about the decay of multilateralism and brought new critical scrutiny to the American exercise of power, but the rest of Ikenberry's analysis remains persuasive today. In the first decade of the new millennium, the preoccupation with American decline in the post-Vietnam War, post-Watergate, oil crisis era of the 1970s—as well as the intellectual controversy set off by Paul Kennedy's thesis about the rise and fall of great powers that spurred a huge debate about American decline in the 1980s[2]—seem echoes of a distant bygone era.[3]

The United States appears to hold the fate of the international system in its hands. It can largely determine the viability of key international treaties and the cornerstone institutions of global governance as well as the geopolitical agendas to be taken up (whether willingly or more coercively) by nation-states around the world. In short, the United States presides over an international order in which the key institutions largely do its bidding, reflect and promulgate the values to which it lays claim, and inspire the diffusion and widespread adoption of "American" values such as liberal democracy, competitiveness, and free trade, which come to appear as natural and inevitable.[4] Today there is no longer much debate about the fact of America's preeminent status as hegemonic power.[5] There is a great deal of debate, however, about the consequences of America's exercise of hegemonic power.

EVALUATING AMERICAN HEGEMONY

In nearly every commentary about the dominant influence of the United States on global politics and economics there is an air of inevitability about America's role, but acknowledgment of both the broad sweep and the depth of American hegemony comes in two versions: in simplest terms there are the *critics* who can only muster a grudging acquiescence when faced with overwhelming evidence of American global dominance and the *boosters* who, try as they might to maintain objectivity, delight in the sway of American power.

It will become clear that the two camps part company decisively in how they might answer our two core questions: (1) how does globalization affect state power? (2) what are the consequences of America's unrivalled power? The critics see a zero-sum game in which state power exercised by the United States tends to crowd out and constrain the exercise of power by other states. Not surprisingly, the boosters see a win-win situation. For them, globalization, in the sway of American leadership, is like a rising tide that raises all ships, enhancing prospects of democracy and prosperity, and encouraging the effective applications of state power by any and all states that recognize the rules of the game.

America's Magnetic Attraction: Two Polar Positions

Few take issue with the claim that the United States dominates the global order. Its hegemony is acknowledged, if ruefully, even by those who by habit, perspective, and national interest might wish that the international system looked a lot more "multipolar" than "unipolar" across all the dimensions of power and influence. Consider the following observation about the preponderant global influence of the United States:

> *Among the 189 countries in the world today, one constitutes a category all by itself. . . . I'm talking about the United States, the world's only "hyperpower." The United States is predominant in all areas: economic, technological, military, monetary, linguistic, cultural. The situation is unprecedented: what previous empire subjugated the entire world, including its adversaries?*[6]

To put this observation in perspective, it was offered by Hubert Védrine, the French foreign minister from 1997 to 2002, in a book entitled *France in an Age of Globalization* that is really a primer on America's global influence. Clearly, the former French foreign minister, even when he puts his best academic and diplomatic gloss on French misgivings, must be counted as a leading critic.

The United States "rules supreme in the waters of globalization," concedes Védrine, noting that the United States (like Britain, its hegemonic forerunner in the nineteenth century) uses its position to pursue an "open door" trade policy. "Americans get great benefits from this for a large number of reasons: because of their economic size; because globalization takes place in their language; because it is organized along neoliberal economic principles; because they impose their legal, accounting, and technical practices; and because they're advocates of individualism."[7]

In Védrine's eyes, there is an overlay of regret mixed with grudging respect, and the inevitable criticisms, explicit and implied, inspired by France's deeply felt global mission as civilizer, diplomatic force, and counter-weight to the U.S. "hyperpower." It should come as no surprise that France would prefer a multipolar world order since a less lopsided geopolitical configuration would preserve a greater sphere of maneuver for France and for the European Union (the expansive regional platform from which France can exert significant global leadership).

But there is more than self-interest or petty rivalry in the French foreign minister's observations about American power and influence. Védrine fears that the ability of the United States to attract others to the American model—the *magnetic attraction* of American power—generates some potentially dangerous consequences. In terms of the scale of influence and universality, for Védrine America is more like the Roman Empire than the British Empire: "American globalism . . . dominates everything everywhere."[8]

Hence, any failures of the American model create worrisome spillover effects. He argues that the American electoral system fails to protect democracy from the influence of money and lobbyists and that a global vision "torn between isolationism and hegemony, weakened by abstention, often hindered by tensions between the White House and Congress . . . is a serious handicap for the United States, and therefore a problem for everyone."[9] Like a real magnetic field, it seems, the force of American hegemony can both attract and repel.

In contrast, Thomas Friedman (a leading booster of U.S. dominated globalization, although he tries to deny it) thinks that there is far less to worry about when it comes to the tightly linked phenomena of American hegemony and globalization. Their magnetic appeal is overwhelmingly positive, almost hypnotic. For Friedman, globalization is as natural as the sun rising and nearly as essential for wellbeing. "Generally speaking, I think it is a good thing that the sun comes up every morning," remarks Friedman. "It does more good than harm, especially if you wear sunscreen and sunglasses."[10] American dominance seems equally natural and foreordained.[11]

It is not quite right, however, to say that the influential *New York Times* op-ed journalist, lecturer, and author thinks that when it comes to globalization there is nothing new under the sun. In comparison to the era of globalization before World War I, the degree of economic integration is far greater. New computer-based technologies transform the way the world does business and the way ordinary people cross boundaries in their lives (apparently Friedman's elderly mother in Minneapolis plays bridge on the Internet with someone in Siberia). The United States has replaced the United Kingdom as the dominant power and like Britain in the earlier era America today makes good use of its dominant position in the global order. "That earlier era was dominated by British power, the British pound and the British navy," wrote Friedman in *The Lexus and the Olive Tree*, comparing the contemporary era of globalization to the period before World War I. "Today's era is dominated by American power, American culture, the American dollar and the American navy."[12]

American influence and strategic design, he argues, was behind the formation of the key institutions of global governance and gave the United States a huge advantage once the current era of globalization blossomed. As Friedman put it, "[W]hen the Information Revolution flowered in the late 1980s—and made it possible for so many more people to act globally, communicate globally, travel globally and sell globally—it flowered into a global power structure that encouraged and enhanced all these trends and made it very costly for any country that tried to buck them."[13]

In Friedman's interpretation of the formation and consolidation of the contemporary international system, globalization has locked in American dominance as a permanent fact of life about global power. And American influence is both benign and pervasive: it forces a market discipline and political responsibility on leaders everywhere, and creates the opportunities (as detailed in Thesis 3) for a virtuous cycle of modernization and democratization on an increasingly developed plane.

Friedman tries to preserve a journalist's proper impartiality about globalization and U.S. power, but fails to persuade on this point, at least. Almost by definition, for Friedman American power and influence has become indistinguishable from globalization. Globalization in turn tends to universalize the virtues of democracy, modernization, and development, virtues for which the United States has achieved the greatest success in global branding.

The magnetic force of American power, charging every particle in its field, attracting and repelling, generates fundamental disagreements about who wins when America rules. For Védrine the United States wins at great peril to others; for Friedman everyone who is willing and able to follow the example set by the United States benefits from globalization in America's image. A chasm divides the critics from the boosters, but these broad-brush treatments have their limits. They clarify the terms of the debate about American hegemony, but do not provide the necessary fine-grained analysis and carefully discriminating argument. To refine the answers to our two core questions about state power and the consequences of American hegemony, we must look more closely at the specific challenges faced by the United States, which reveal its sources of unrivaled power, its vulnerabilities, and its capacity to mold the global order to do its bidding—up to a point.

A DAY IN THE LIFE OF A HEGEMONIC POWER

How pervasive is American influence over the forces of globalization from economic integration to the configuration of geopolitical power? How well is America doing as the mover, shaker, and shaper of globalization? And, finally, what does the unique global role of the United States mean for American national politics? One day in the life of the last remaining superpower (November 19, 2003) as described in the pages of perhaps the world's leading daily for globalization news, the London-based *Financial Times,* reveals quite a lot about the challenges America faces in the global age.

It was by no means a slow news day in London. President Bush was beginning the first full day of his historic visit to the United Kingdom (the first official state visit by an American president in more than 80 years) by breakfasting with the Queen at Buckingham Palace. Meanwhile, the tabloids were going mad about the cost of the visit, including 14,000 shifts by London's Metropolitan Police, who were bracing for sizeable demonstrations against the war in Iraq and operating on high alert due to the increased risk of terror attacks.

By any standard the high visibility meeting between two leaders under political fire for the war in Iraq to discuss the way forward—set against the backdrop of intensified resistance to Anglo-American occupation in Iraq—was a huge story in London. Nevertheless, the *Financial Times* (which in the preceding weeks often gave pride of place in coverage to the war in Iraq and its domestic fallout) led with the headline: "Dollar hits record low against euro."[14] The story blamed the weakening dollar on the release of U.S. Treasury figures indicating a precipitous decline in the net inflow of foreign capital to the United States. Although a monthly dip, however steep, cannot demonstrate a trend, a drop from $50 billion in September to $4.2 billion in October (the lowest monthly figure since 1998) raised concerns about the size and consequences of the current account deficit that averaged $48 billion a month for the first half of 2003. As one currency analyst put it, "The September data is the strongest evidence to date that the record US current account deficit has become too large to finance through the net foreign investment into US securities."[15]

Just below the lead story was one with a Washington dateline about the decision by the Bush administration to impose unprecedented restrictions in the form of quotas on several varieties of apparel and textile imports from China.[16] The two stories are connected and, taken together, they underscore what many consider one of the most worrisome aspects of American vulnerability in an interdependent global economy. The United States has become increasingly reliant on the inflow of foreign capital to offset American's chronic trade deficit.

That same day's news included discouraging new data from the annual "Cyberstates" survey of high-technology industry by the American Electronic Association, which projected three-quarters of a million high-technology jobs lost in the United States in 2002–2003. Although the rate of job loses was slowing, the effect of the downturn since the Internet bubble burst in 2002 was quite dramatic: about 12 percent of the total jobs in the high-tech sector at the end of 2001 were gone.[17] At the same time, high-tech exports—which still represented nearly one-quarter of all U.S. exports—fell by 12 percent in 2002.[18]

AMERICAN VULNERABILITIES EXPOSED

What does this story (as it continues to unfold) tell us about the power and influence of the United States, its ability to mold the global order to its purposes, and the domestic repercussions of global interdependence—and unwelcome global vulnerabilities?

A somber picture emerges from this day in the life of the American hegemon: gigantic trade and budget deficits, the flare-up of endemic trade wars facing the United States with key trading partners, the well-founded fears of job-losses in key sectors of the American economy, a growing vulnerability to "inflationary collapse" if China or other deep-pocket, big-surplus countries decided to ratchet down their willingness to fund the American deficit for any reason (whether due to their own domestic political considerations or due to objections to U.S. foreign policy or trade policy).

It has taken some time for the new facts of life to filter through America's self-image as kingmaker and "workshop of the world" in the global age. Is globalization "Made in America"? Have a look at the label in the clothes or the shoes you are wearing: you are a lot more likely to see "Made in China" (or in Indonesia or the Philippines or Slovakia) than "Made in America"—or so it seems in textile towns in places like North Carolina where a great many people feel the pinch of foreign imports, fear worse, and let the politicians know it. Likewise, the job losses and slumping economic fortunes in California, home to America's embattled high-tech capital Silicon Valley, have tremendous political repercussions. Global interdependence cuts many ways.

For better or worse, there is nothing new in American trade deficits and the vulnerabilities they expose. Since 1995, when the U.S. Treasury shifted its dollar policy to push up the value of the dollar against the yen and the mark, there has been a surge in imports (since a high dollar policy lowers the cost to American consumers of imported products) and a corresponding increase in America's trade deficit. By 2000, the steadily rising trade deficit amounted to a huge 1.5 percent of world gross domestic product (GDP).[19] What is newer is the exposure this deficit represents. Despite the powerful up tick in the U.S. economy in the fourth quarter of 2003, grounds for concern remained about how sound the fundamentals of the American economy may be.

Robust growth, a recovering stock market, and some good news on job growth provided positive auguries through the winter and spring of 2004. But the growing deficit raised widespread concern, the weak dollar created endless copy for editorial writers and political spinners in the run up to the November 2004 election, rising interest rates beginning in spring 2004 increased the anxiety levels for many Americans who were nearly maxed out on credit cards and stretched by mortgage payments (often with variable rates), and sluggish job growth in June and July raised doubts about the recovery. "[T]he twin U.S. budget and trade deficits would set alarm bells ringing if we were a third world country," wrote Paul Krugman, economist turned op-ed writer and Administration critic in *The New York Times*. "For now, America gets the benefit of the doubt, but if financial markets decide that we have turned into a banana republic, the sky's the limit for interest rates."[20]

The budget and trade deficits have become an important nexus where global economic interdependence and partisan domestic politics come together to produce deepening vulnerabilities. Needless to say, all these concerns about deepening economic vulnerabilities that straddle the domestic and international domains are magnified by fears of a trade war between the United States and China. Seizing the initiative, China wasted no time in blasting the American decision to impose quotas, saying it "runs against WTO principles of free trade, transparency and non-discrimination."[21] Given both the sensitivity and significance of U.S./China relations, the news of intensified strains over trade policy assumed importance well beyond the limited scope of the new restrictions (which covered less than 5 percent of the $10 billion annual Chinese imports to the United States in clothing and textiles alone).[22]

While this trade controversy was being played out, the United States also had to reckon with the domestic and geopolitical repercussions of a trade war on another front. Playing to domestic constituencies in politically crucial industrial states, in March 2002 Bush had unveiled with considerable fanfare a decision to impose a set of duties of up to 30 percent on some steel imports. Predictably, the policy hurt steel-consuming industries in the United States (such as automobile manufacturing) and infuriated steel-exporting trade partners. The EU, Japan, South Korea, China, Norway, New Zealand, Switzerland, and Brazil challenged the U.S. tariffs at the World Trade Organization, arguing that these steel tariffs violated international trade rules. In November 2003, the WTO's appellate body affirmed an earlier ruling against the United States.

The Bush administration was then faced with an unusually determined stance by a host of trading partners lead by the EU to wield massive WTO-approved retaliatory tariffs on a range of carefully selected products targeted to hurt the president's chances in swing states in November 2004, including such states as Florida, Ohio, Virginia, and Pennsylvania. Bush backed down and eliminated the American steel tariffs in December 2003. But even with one key front in the all but perpetual trade wars between the United States and the European Union taken out of the battle, another opened up.

On March 1, 2004, for the first time ever, the European Union imposed trade sanctions on the United States for their failure to repeal a law that gives tax breaks to U.S. exporters, which was ruled illegal by the WTO in 2002. Then, in April 2004, the EU announced plans to retaliate against the United States for a WTO violation again (the Byrd Amendment, which permits the proceeds of antidumping duties and antisubsidies duties to be passed onto the companies that initially brought the complaint). Showing their determination—and political savvy—once again, the EU targeted the same states as they had in the steel dispute, and the same industries that might prove particularly sensitive to trade pressures and show their displeasure in November: textiles, tobacco, clothes and shoes, fruit, vegetables, and rice.[23]

Meanwhile, the U.S./China front remained exposed, although there were signs in April 2004 that the United States and China were taking steps to ease tensions, resolve disputes, reduce the trade deficit, and blunt charges that competition from China was hurting the American workforce.[24] This new commitment to resolve disputes, sustained mostly by Chinese concessions, suggests that the strategic stakes in this bilateral relationship in both economic and geopolitical terms have become higher than ever. (The growing significance of and shifting balance in U.S./China relations will be discussed further in Chapter 4).

Beyond the importance of specific bilateral relationships, the trade disputes with China over textiles and apparel, the controversies with the EU and a host of trading partners about steel—and the news in April 2004 that Brazil won the first round at the WTO in a dispute over subsidies to American cotton farmers—reveal some important truths about state power in the era of globalization.

These trade disputes provide indisputable evidence that even the ranking hegemon is not free of the constraints of negotiated sovereignty imposed by multi-level governance. When Bush backed down in the face of retaliatory tariffs when the WTO affirmed its judgment against the United States in the steel dispute, it became clear both in the United States and around the world that even the United States can be subjected to the will of the WTO, a key institution in the architecture of global governance. Like the "Butterfly Effect" ascribed to Edward Lorenz, in which the flap of a butterfly's wings in Brazil could set off a Tornado in Texas, when Bush blinked in the steel case it had global repercussions.

Brazil was emboldened, as would be other states bringing claims against the United States, by the knowledge that victory at the WTO was achievable—and

American climbdowns in advance of aggressive and politically astute retaliatory tariffs were to be expected. It is also very clear that global trade politics has become national and local politics in the United States. If the cotton ruling is upheld and if, as some observers expect, it opens the door to broader challenges to agricultural subsidies, American farmers (who have come to depend on $19 billion annual farm subsidies) will notice—and critical votes in Farm Belt states, which Republicans rely upon, may turn into swing votes.[25] Hence we can expect that trade politics about steel, agriculture, or outsourcing, will turn heads on main street—and may shape voting behavior in swing states at election time.

When it comes to economic interdependence (and recalling our core questions), the vulnerabilities reflected in trade deficits, reliance on China and other big-surplus countries to fund the budget deficit, and subjection to WTO rulings all point to an important conclusion. Even for the United States, globalization limits the capacity of the state to secure desirable outcomes and effectively shape the behavior of other states and social actors. The facts of life of economic interdependence provide strong corroboration, as well, for Thesis 2, which emphasizes that as powerful as it is, the United States is not immune from the constrains imposed by the necessity to operate through inter-state negotiations and the arrangements imposed by multi-level governance.

AMERICAN POWER: DOMINANT
BUT NOT OMNIPOTENT[26]

As Védrine conceded, "the United States rules supreme in the waters of globalization."[27] Taken together, however, the symbiotic terms of U.S./China relations, the endemic trade wars, mounting trade and budget deficits, and the declining fortunes and job losses suffered by U.S. manufacturing from the textile mills of the South to the high technology meccas of Silicon Valley all begin to suggest that there is another more vulnerable side to American hegemony. Above we examined the contour's of American vulnerability associated with global economic independence and the resulting constraints that are imposed on its autonomous control over policy outcomes. But the notion of American economic vulnerability—or indeed that of significant constraints on its policy or its geopolitical sphere of maneuver—should not be exaggerated.

The *US Global Profile* suggests the magnetic attraction of the United States, which brings nearly half-a-million students annually to study in America. It also reveals both a highly integrated economy, with imports accounting for nearly one-seventh of the country's GDP and—at over 15 percent of total government spending—the massive commitment to the military capability needed to sustain geopolitical dominance. Whatever disagreements there may be about the status and role of the America as global hegemon (even empire), this much is beyond dispute: the United States is the dominant player in global economic competition and the unrivaled geopolitical power. Neither its newly exposed vulnerabilities

FIGURE 2.1
US Global Profile

Economic Integration	Political Integration
U.S. — bar chart: Exports of Goods and Services as % of GDP (2000) = 10.72; Imports of Goods and Services as % of GDP (2000) = 13.47; Foreign Direct Investment (2000) = 2.92; y-axis %GDP	Number of diplomatic missions in U.S. 163 Number of U.S. diplomatic mission abroad 142 • Joined the United Nations in 1945. • Kyoto Protocol not ratified. • Convention on the Elimination of All forms of Discrimination against Women not ratified.

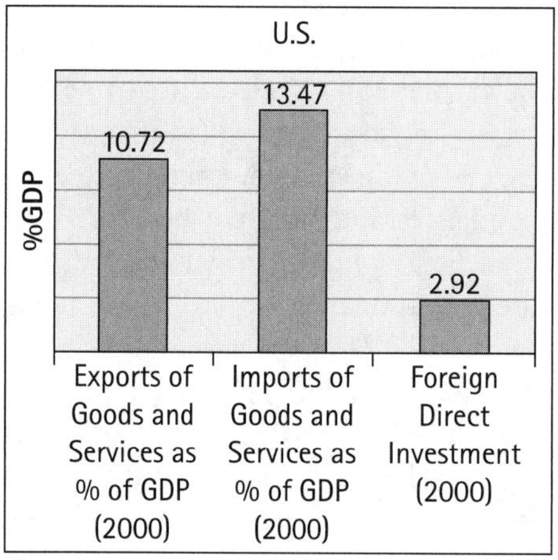

Information Flows	Cultural Influences
International mail (letters per person per year sent or received from abroad) 1997 9 International phone calls (outgoing minutes per person per year) 1997 85	Percentage of population foreign born (1990–1995) 7.9 Imported feature films as percentage of total films distributed (1994–1998) 42

People Flows	Security and Military Interaction
Number of students abroad/number of foreign students (thousand) 1994–1997: American students abroad 30.4 thousand Foreign students in U.S. 454.8 thousand	Military expenditure as percentage of government spending 15.70 Arms exports (percentage of total exports) 4.7 Arms imports (percentage of total imports) 0.2

nor the concessions it must make, however reluctantly, to the facts of life of multi-level governance undercut the status of the United States as hegemon. Rather they affirm the universality of interdependence in the global age, while they preserve the familiar order of things.

Competitiveness Where it Counts

There seems to be a growing consensus that the competitiveness that matters most for advanced economies is competitiveness in knowledge driven sectors where the quality of goods (more than the price of goods) is the primary source of competitive advantage.[28] "For high-income economies at this Innovation-Driven stage of economic development, global competitiveness is critically linked to high rates of social learning (especially science-based learning) and the rapid ability to shift to new technologies," states the recent World Economic Forum report on global competitiveness. "Successful economic development is thus a process of successive upgrading, in which businesses and their supporting environments co-evolve, to foster increasingly sophisticated ways of producing and competing."[29]

Highly successful advanced economies should be particularly strong in their global share of high-technology exports and in this dimension the United States dominates, with more than one-quarter of the world's total.[30] Figures 2.2, 2.3, and 2.4 indicate in stark graphic terms the level of American leadership in telecommunications equipment and in semiconductors and its dominance in aircraft and spacecraft sectors. The 2002–2003 World Economic Forum report on global competitiveness places the United States number one in the world in its Technology Index and Growth Competitiveness Index rankings. (The Growth Competitiveness Index is based on an ensemble of variables that are considered

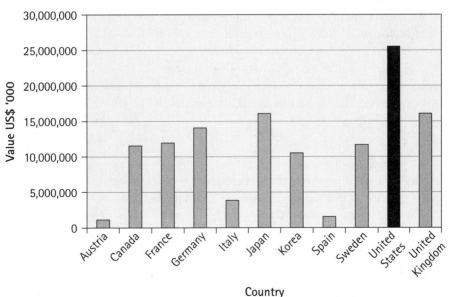

FIGURE 2.2
Exports of Telecommunications Equipment in 2000

Source: ITC Databases: International Trade Statistics (764).

FIGURE 2.3
Exports of Aircraft and Spacecraft Equipment in 2000

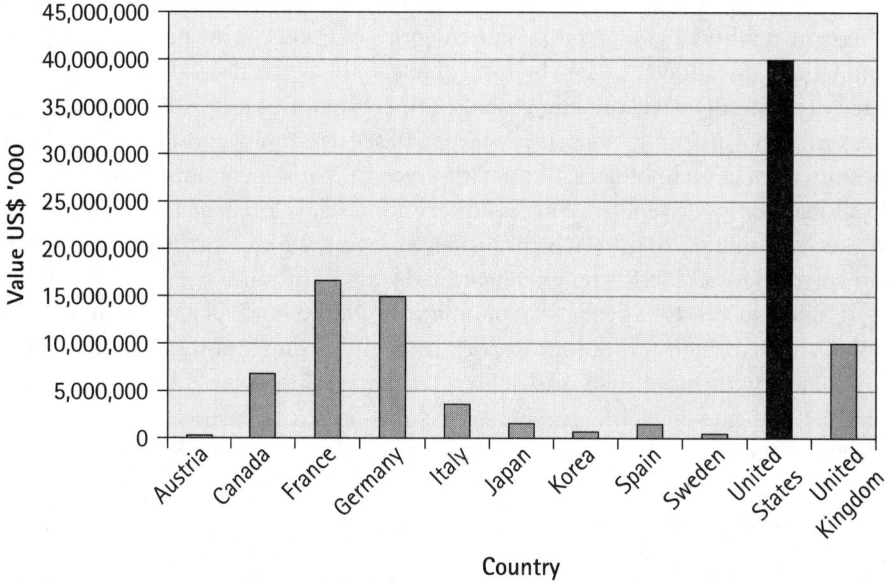

Source: ITC Databases: International Trade Statistics (792).

the drivers behind economic growth in the medium as well as the long term, including factors related to the performance of public institutions, the qualities of the macroeconomic environment, and technological progress and innovation).[31]

In its national competitiveness balance sheet, the United States also scores first in several technology measures including "technological sophistication" and in "company spending on research and development." Also among America's notable competitive advantages may be found first place rankings in six dimensions of microeconomic competitiveness identified in the report:

1. Sophistication of Company Operations
   • Extent of marketing
   • Degree of Customer orientation
   • Extent of incentive compensation
2. Quality of the National Business Environment
   • Venture capital availability
   • Utility patents
   • Intensity of local competition

If these signs of U.S. superiority in key indicators of technological innovation and firm behavior come as no surprise, neither do several competitive disadvantages of the United States that are also identified by the report. Among these may

FIGURE 2.4

Exports of Valves, Transistors, and Semiconductor Devices in 2000

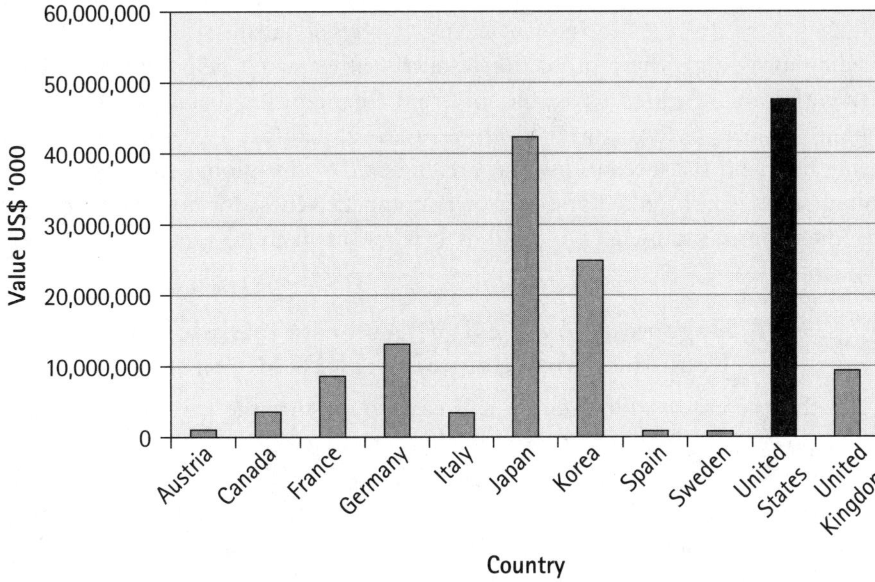

Source: ITC Databases: International Trade Statistics (776).

be found: national savings rate (ranked 75), prevalence of foreign technology licensing (63), investment rate, 2001 (71), exports, 2001 (79). Perhaps most predictably, strong negative competitive indicators included: military expenditure relative to central government expenditure (64), business costs of terrorism (74), and compliance with international environmental agreements (58). The quality of public schools (29) and math and science education (38), access to credit (48) and efficiency of the tax system (38) must also be included among the notable competitive disadvantages that characterize the U.S. economy.[32]

However, on balance, the exhaustive research behind the *Global Competitiveness Report* confirms the overall dominance of the U.S. economy, a key attribute of its hegemonic standing. The American economy is especially strong where it counts, in knowledge-driven quality-competitive, high-tech sectors. It exhibits tremendous strength in microeconomic behavior, unrivaled excellence in the sophistication of firm operations, and unsurpassed strengths in its business environment. These drivers of economic development and competitiveness are more than enough to provide an optimistic reading of future competitiveness, and in the current period (through the second quarter of 2004) the United States has exhibited the economic growth trajectory to back up the analysis.

But trade deficits, massive job losses in key manufacturing sectors, which include very significant losses in the knowledge-driven, high-tech industries, and the reduced value of the dollar, matter as well in both economic and political terms. These developments reveal imbalances in the American economy that are intensified by global economic competition. They also signal political challenges that may have a life of their own in any congressional district where jobs are bleeding away and where protectionist tariffs either won't help enough or have been withdrawn. As jobs across the spectrum are migrating (being "outsourced") in huge numbers to lower wage locations in the global factory, voters are experiencing firsthand the insecurities that are endemic to this global age. Clearly, the United States is not ranked first in growth competitiveness for no reason, and yet the American economy, as powerful as it is and is likely to remain, is far from invincible.

Hegemony By Design? America's Global Economic and Geopolitical Dominance

In this the era of globalization it is easy to see that the various domains of global power and influence are interactive and overlapping. Because it is the hegemonic power, almost by definition, the United States benefits disproportionately from the design of the institutions of global economic and political governance. Thus, a mutually reenforcing logic has tended to enhance American power. The formative role of the United States as fledging hegemon in the post-World War II era provided it with the tools to shape the institutions of global governance that emerged in this period; these institutions in turn have safeguarded American interests ever since and helped consolidate both the international order bequeathed by the United States and America's dominant role in that order. This is the core premise of Thesis 1 (the invisible hand thesis).

Even erstwhile critics recognize that there is nothing sinister in this pattern of snowballing hegemony. As Védrine explained America's unprecedented dominance in every area (including economic, military, technological, and cultural), he acknowledged "while U.S. domination may be the result of a project . . . it is certainly not the result of a plot."[33] No conspiracy theory is required in order to recognize that hegemony is anchored and enhanced by a set of multilateral institutions that serve American interests.

Explanations vary in interesting and important ways about how and why the hegemonic order dominated by the United States was consolidated. For example, Robert Hunter Wade downplays the intentionality or grand vision associated with American hegemony and emphasizes the snowballing advantages of an "international economic architecture" that buttresses the geopolitical and economic power of the United States through the invisible hand of global market forces.[34] In an argument to which we will return in Chapter 6 when we discuss Thesis 1, Wade describes the bountiful advantages that flow to the United States from an international financial architecture that gives the United States uniquely autonomous and powerful tools of statecraft to control foreign exchange markets.

Hence, argues Wade, the rest of the world is harnessed to the economic rhythms of the United States, and the United States alone possesses the ability to adjust exchange rates for domestic political goals or to hurt competitors. Not only can the hegemonic power pull the levers to advance its interests with reference to financial markets and international trade, it can also use its dominance in the arenas of global governance to good effect. It can advance parochial policy aims, while gaining the benefits of political cover associated with participation as one among many in multilateral institutions. "To supervise this international framework you need a flotilla of international organizations that look like cooperatives of member states and confer the legitimacy of multilateralism, but that you can control by setting the rules and blocking outcomes you don't like,"[35] observes Wade in an argument reminiscent of Joseph Stiglitz's critique of U.S. dominance of the WTO and the IMF.[36]

In the end, the architectural design of American hegemony is both powerful and elegant, forcing others to accede to U.S. interests, yet concealing as best it can the principles of construction that might offend visitors from abroad who might prefer a more balanced multipolar system. This is how Wade describes the bottom line of U.S. dominance along the road to a new American Empire:

> *This international economic architecture allows your people to consume far more than they produce; it allows your firms and your capital to enter and exit other markets quickly, maximizing short-run returns; it locks in net flows of technology rents from the rest of the world for decades ahead and thereby boosts incentives for your firms to innovate; and through market forces seemingly free of political power it reinforces your geopolitical dominance over other states. All the better if your social scientists explain to the public that a structureless and agentless process of globalization—the relentless technological change that shrinks time and distance—is behind all this, causing all states, including your own, to lose power vis-à-vis markets. You do not want others to think that globalization within the framework you have constructed raises your ability to have both a large military and prosperous civilian sector while diminishing everyone else's.[37]*

Of course, not everyone agrees that the bottom line of U.S. hegemony is a beggar everyone else outcome, that the resulting dominance has given rise to an imperial America, or that the consolidation of U.S. hegemony is best explained by a combination of the invisible-hand of markets and the whip hand of blatant American self-interest projected onto the global arena.

In striking contrast to Wade, G. John Ikenberry argues that American hegemony was built on a set of principles that articulated a compelling vision for liberal hegemony expressed in a nondiscriminatory free trading system, democratic governance, and the institutions to regulate both. And there was nothing much invisible about it. Ikenberry argues, in fact, that American hegemony was the product of two rather explicit postwar settlements and that the United States was able to advance its vision of the international order because America's vision was able to resolve a crucial problem: "how to build a durable and mutually acceptable order among a group of states with huge power asymmetries."[38]

The pair of settlements (or tacit agreements about the era's institutionalized arrangements) that helped to shape, define and justify the broad policies, institutions, and values of the postwar order varied in specificity and scope. The more sharply drawn and acutely focused of the two was the "containment order" that consecrated the Cold War: a wary balance of power backed by nuclear deterrence and animated by ideological and geopolitical competition. More sweeping, but also more diffuse, was the broader vision for a liberal democratic order. It was also more American in design and purpose, as Ikenberry observes, than was recognized at the time:

> *The liberal democratic agenda was built on a robust and sophisticated set of ideas about American security interests, the causes of war and depression, and the proper and desirable foundations of postwar political order. Indeed, although the containment order overshadowed it, the ideas behind postwar liberal democratic order were more deeply rooted in the American experience and a thoroughgoing understanding of history, economics, and the sources of political order.*[39]

American policy-makers made the case that free trade, an open trading system, and a set of multilateral institutions was in the broader interests of Western democracies. Ikenberry argues that it was a case that could be sold convincingly to Asian and European partners because the United States was satisfied to "lock in" the terms of these favorable settlements, preferring stability and predictability to the uncertainty of an unconstrained hegemonic order in which the United States might aggrandize even greater power. To use Mearsheimer's framework, the United States exhibited the tendencies of defensive rather than offensive realism.[40] Ikenberry argues that the willingness of the United States to exercise "strategic restraint"—and persuade potential partners of their commitment to the principles of a noncoercive and multilateral postwar order—were essential to achieving a durable settlement. In short, "the United States gained the acquiescence of secondary states by accepting limits on the exercise of its own hegemonic power."[41]

Who wins when America rules? Wade and Ikenberry are sharply at odds. Wade argues that when America rules, every one else loses in a zero-sum game played by rules that inevitably enhance U.S. power at the expense of every other state. In stark contrast, Ikenberry argues that American hegemony was built on a set of commonly held liberal democratic principles. The postwar order was anchored by a pair of settlements that were honorably negotiated by a hegemonic power, which was more interested in stability than domination. By this account, which bears much kinship with Thesis 3 (globalization as the engine of democracy and progress), when America rules it attracts other states into a win-win partnership and enhances a global project for democratic stability. Although divergent in their interpretations of the postwar hegemonic order and the role and function of American power, Wade and Ikenberry would probably find ready agreement in the proposition that 9/11 and the emergence of the Bush doctrine heightened the willingness of the United States to project power in a far less restrained manner, a theme to which we now turn.

From Magnetic to Irresistible Force?

As we will discuss further in Chapter 5, after the terror attacks of September 11, 2001, and with the emergence of the Bush revolution in foreign policy, America's rules of engagement with the rest of the world changed rather dramatically. First, because the nation faced terrible new dangers, the United States took the reasonable position that it could not rely on others to protect its people or safeguard its borders. This belief won very broad support at home and an extremely sympathetic hearing abroad. It went the more controversial step further of asserting that the United States could not afford to be constrained by multilateral institutions.

What was even more revolutionary and unsettling for many was the second belief enshrined in the emerging Bush foreign policy doctrine, as Ivo H. Daalder and James M. Lindsay put it "that an America unbound should use its strength to change the status quo in the world."[42] As a result, the emerging Bush doctrine argued that the United States should "go abroad searching for monsters to destroy."[43] At a stroke, Bush unilaterally abrogated the terms of the postwar settlement described by Ikenberry that had anchored liberal hegemony and stabilized the international order.

For more than a half-century, the leadership of the United States was entrenched in a rule-bound system of international law and global governance that limited the prerogatives of the weak as well as the powerful. Paradoxically, American strength and global authority was enhanced by its willingness to accept limits on the exercise of its hegemonic privileges, and a stable order was secured. Philip Stephens, a columnist in the *Financial Times*, has articulated very clearly the dangers associated with a transformation of U.S. foreign policy doctrine that erodes the principles of the post-World War II geopolitical and security order:

> *That order, entrenched in the UN and Bretton Woods systems, in Nato and in a panoply of multilateral treaties, may now be too badly broken to fix. Mr Bush's national security strategy, with its emphasis on unfettered US power, has replaced rules-based leadership with imperial hegemony. I sympathise with the idea that structures shaped by the cold war have lost some of their relevance. But the underlying choice for the US is as it was in 1945: does it exercise its leadership co-operatively or coercively? Mr Bush has made his choice.*[44]

In geopolitical and military terms, the United States remains unrivaled and faces no serious contenders for state dominance. That does not mean, however, that the exercise of American power is unrestrained. As competitive and dominant in key, high-tech sectors as the U.S. economy remains, the changing terms of U.S./China relations, trade wars on several fronts, and the loss of some two-and-a-half-million manufacturing jobs in the first three years of the twenty-first century reveal new vulnerabilities—and demonstrate that even the sole hyperpower is not immune to competitive pressures or wholly free of the constraints imposed on all states by powerful international organizations such as the WTO.

It seems that in the post-9/11 era, the United States has forsaken the self-imposed strategic restraint described by Ikenberry. For how long and to what purpose will the United States assume the potentially more dangerous geopolitical posture of an imperial power? Is this more aggressive approach the necessary but temporary response to the new security threats of this woeful era, with the United States likely to revert to the post-1945 strategic restraint doctrine when the insecurities of 9/11 have been reduced to a more acceptable level? Or are we entering a new phase of geopolitics in which the United States doesn't simply exert a magnetic force—attracting some and repelling others—but becomes an irresistible force, willing to turn the international order upside down in order to control the global agenda to advance its national interests? We will discuss the implications of this turn toward a new American empire in Chapter 6.

Deeply held convictions about America's ultimate role in the global era turn on the answers to these questions, just as the fate of presidencies in the years ahead may turn in large measure on the electorate's assessment of an administration's success in managing the domestic consequences of globalization as they have come to be measured in terms of homeland security, employment and competitiveness, and the capacity of those representing the United States to work effectively in the economic and political institutions of global governance.

Undoubtedly, globalization and the power of the U.S. state are intertwined in a kind of Gordian knot, the fate of the United States and the future of global politics, more tightly bound together than ever before. What we don't know is whether—or under what circumstances—the Gordian knot may be loosened. And there is little agreement about whether that would be a good or bad thing. But this much is clear as we proceed to an analysis of the global challenges facing Europe: the problem posed by power asymmetries has returned with a vengeance, and the need for a fresh political settlement to consolidate and justify a new international political order is very much back on the table.

CHAPTER 3

Can Europe Still Be Europe?

Early in the spring of 2003, as UN inspectors searched for weapons of mass destruction in a desperate race against time, troubling divisions between the United States and Europe and equally significant divisions within Europe spilled out into the open. The Atlantic alliance and the prospects for a cohesive and independent European foreign policy were thus the first casualties of the war yet to be fought.

As France and Germany led the campaign to deny Security Council approval for the Anglo-American plans for invasion and regime change in Iraq, a host of other European countries (the "Euro 8" quickly followed by the "Vilnius 10") took the unusual step of going public with op-ed statements scattered across Europe in support of the U.S. position at the United Nations.* Timed to correspond with Secretary of State Colin Powell's dramatic appeal to the Security Council in early February that "facts" not "assertions" made regime change imperative, the statement was intended to show European support for the U.S. position that the world must disarm Saddam Hussein, by force if necessary.

But the statements did much more than that. They revealed multiple divisions within Europe that may outlast the U.S./European rift over the war in Iraq, and have far reaching consequences for the future of the European Union.

Within Europe, there were divisions over America's insistence on regime change as well as its open threat to wage war without United Nations endorsement. Disagreements over the tenor of support for the uncompromising posture of the United States were significant enough to limit the scope of the endorsement expressed in the unusual advocacy campaign by the pro-American European leaders. Although the statement by the Vilnius Group soon took on legendary proportions, few bothered to peruse the text carefully, but in this case what was not said may be as important as what was said.

---

*The open letter from the "Euro 8" was issued on January 30, 2003, signed by the presidents or prime ministers of the Czech Republic, Denmark, Hungary, Italy, Poland, Spain, and the United Kingdom. The Vilnius Group response to and support for Colin Powell's statement to the United Nations Security Council, issued on February 5, 2003, was signed by the foreign ministers of Albania, Bulgaria, Croatia, Estonia, Latvia, Lithuania, Macedonia, Romania, Slovakia, and Slovenia.

The statement signed by the Vilnius 10 affirmed, "The trans-Atlantic community, of which we are a part, must stand together to face the threat posed by the nexus of terrorism and dictators with weapons of mass destruction."[1] The Vilnius 10 also affirmed support for UN Security Council resolution 1441 that declared Iraq in material breach of prior resolutions, insisted on Iraq's full disclosure of weapons of mass destruction, and required that Iraq fully cooperate with the UN inspectors or risk "serious consequences" that would surely entail the use of force. Although the statement was usually depicted as providing blanket support for the U.S. position and also for the imminent invasion of Iraq, the statement did not endorse war without Security Council support nor did it explicitly embrace regime change.

Perhaps more significant, the unprecedented op-ed campaign for a tough stance on Iraq revealed a deep public rift between all the signatories to the statement supporting Colin Powell's approach on the one side, and the French and Germans who tried with great determination to turn Europe against the United States on the other side. As one respected European observer characterized the subtext and broader significance of the pair of statements in support of the U.S. policy on Iraq: "We are not amused that Paris and Berlin are trying to gang up on the United States in the name of Europe."[2]

The breach within Europe was then unforgettably crystallized in Secretary of Defense Donald Rumsfeld's dismissal of the United State's erstwhile great power allies as "Old Europe," and his observation, "If you look at the entire NATO Europe today, the center of gravity is shifting to the east."[3] Rumsfeld's comments may be self-serving in that they put the best face on a very public row between the United States and European powers (not only France and Germany, but Russia as well). Also, the case could certainly be made that France, Germany, and the United Kingdom anchor European security and dominate EU policy, come what may, and are not likely to be outmuscled or outmaneuvered any time soon by the former communist-party states in the region.

But Rumsfeld also made a telling observation about the direction in which the political winds were blowing, in both NATO and the EU. Poland, Hungary, and the Czech Republic were admitted to NATO in 1999. At the NATO summit in Prague in November 2002, seven additional Eastern and Central European countries were invited to join the Alliance.[†] Similarly, the European Union was moving eastward on a fast track, with eight of the ten new 2004 members coming from Eastern and Central Europe.[‡] The geographical center of gravity in both

---

[†]The countries invited to join NATO were: Bulgaria, Estonia, Latvia, Lithuania, Romania, Slovakia, and Slovenia.
[‡]The eight Eastern and Central European countries admitted in 2004 were: the Czech Republic, Estonia, Hungary, Latvia, Lithuania, Poland, Slovakia, and Slovenia. Cyprus and Malta joined the EU simultaneously, expanding the Union from 15 to 25 members.

NATO and the European Union was moving to the east. America's magnetic attraction to former communist-party states, enhanced by hegemonic hard ball politics, might very well tip the balance of power in both NATO and the European Union in a direction Washington might find very much to its liking.

In this regard it is at least worth noting two additional points. First, every single country slated for either NATO or European Union enlargement signed either the "Euro 8" or the "Vilnius 10" letter of support of the United State's initiatives at the UN in the run up to the war in Iraq. Second, the formal accession protocols governing the admission of seven additional Eastern and Central European countries to NATO were signed within a week of the start of the war in Iraq. Was it coincidence or political hardball?

Rumsfeld widened the breach with "Old Europe" (or to be more accurate France and Germany) by rubbing its face in the apparent fact that the United States had a huge chunk of the former Soviet bloc in its pocket. Even more significant, Rumsfeld placed out in the open for the whole world to see the prospect that not only in NATO but also in the European Union, where France and Germany were viewed almost by right as the dominant powers, things were about to change. The United States could not join Europe, but it could dominate Europe when crossed. The gloves were off in both diplomatic and strategic terms, restraint was no longer the watchword, and the United States was prepared to shuffle the deck.

In his war of words with "Old Europe" Rumsfeld provided a characteristically unvarnished answer to our second core question about the consequences of the U.S. exercise of hegemonic power for other states. When push comes to shove, America will do the shoving. Whether exercised directly or through key international institutions such as NATO and the European Union, American power will remain paramount. It will limit the exercise of power by other states, even the most powerful European states.

It comes as no surprise that Rumsfeld's remark struck a deep nerve of unease in Europe about the destiny of a European Union poised for massive expansion eastward and underscored the fragility of Europe as a geopolitical player. Arguing that the round of U.S./European dust-ups in the period leading to the war in Iraq were decisively won by the United States, Josef Joffe, editor of the German weekly *Die Ziet,* observed: "The real significance of the drama is the collapse of European's pretensions to an independent, let alone cohesive, foreign policy."[4]

Was Joffe premature in his assessment—or is Europe (the European Union), under the watchful and strategically jealous gaze of the United States, destined to remain less than the sum of its parts? Will the American exercise of power to advance its own interest serve to frustrate the aspirations of European unity, prosperity, and greater regional influence that animate EU integration and expansion? Is Rumsfeld's answer right, that the exercise of American power is at the expense of Europe?

THE CLASH OF CIVILIZATIONS?

Tony Judt observes that when a country is slated for membership in the European Union, people "quite simply and unblushingly speak of a country . . . joining Europe."[5] But upon gaining membership on May 1, 2004, what did the eight new Central and Eastern European countries (as well as Cyprus and Malta) join? They joined a single market encompassing 450 million citizens and they entered an immensely complex institutional matrix that is the most developed expression of multi-level government in the world and easily the most confounding.

But, accession to the European Union is both less and more than joining the European Union, accepting a set of treaty obligations, receiving many thousands of pages of directives, and gaining access to important material advantages. It is, in common parlance, "joining Europe," assuming a sensibility, taking on a mission, joining a civilization.

As Judt observes:

> *This curious locution shows how much Europe today is not so much a place as an idea, a peaceful, prosperous, international community of shared interests and collaborating parts; a "Europe of the mind," human rights, of the free movement of goods, ideas, and persons, of ever-greater cooperation and unity. The emergence of this hyper-real Europe, more European than the continent itself, [is] an inward and future projection of all the higher values of . . . civilization but shorn of its darker qualities.*[6]

The actually existing real-time Europe, the Europe facing fierce competitive pressures, beset by xenophobic undercurrents, and trapped in a hopelessly complicated institutional architecture, doesn't look very much like the "hyper-real" glorified image of Europe described above. It is important to come to terms with the distinction between the idealized image of Europe and its far messier realities.

Divisions within Europe

Because Europe and the European Union involve more than markets and institutions, the divisions within Europe run very deep. There are divisions between insiders and outsiders, the dominant EU power brokers from the prosperous West and the humbled petitioners for entry from the previously subjugated and still suspect East, who have been obliged to accept conditions of entry not of their own choosing.

Then there is the fundamental challenge of forging a union that can transcend the division writ large in the "clash of civilizations" logic made famous by Samuel Huntington.[7] As Tariq Modood has observed, "For centuries eastern and central Europe have been a battleground and frontier between Christian peoples and rulers, and Muslim peoples and rulers."[8] Whatever one might think about the validity of Huntington's core claim that the central axis of conflict is determined by fundamental cultural differences that divide Western and non-Western civilizations,[9] it is intriguing to consider how a similar fault line shapes insider/outsider status and animates xenophobia within Europe itself. As Judt certainly recognizes, the notion of a "Europe of the mind" amounts to a rather suspect and exclusionary claim that Europe is a territory and a sensibility defined by a particular set of social, cultural, and civic virtues. Thus European culture is represented as the hallmark of civilization.

In short, this "hyper-real" Europe is a Camelot of Western and Christian civilization. During the Cold War, the geopolitical division between east and west within Europe inevitably took precedence over other far older and, in an important sense, more entrenched divisions. "It is sometimes supposed, today, that the line dividing eastern and western Europe was an artificial creation of the Cold War, an iron curtain gratuitously and recently drawn across a single cultural space," notes Judt. "This is not the case. In the nineteenth century, long after the Habsburg rulers had established effective authority over territories stretching into today's Ukraine, the Austrian Chancellor Metternich could famously speak of Asia as beginning at the *Landstrasse,* the road leading east out of Vienna."[10]

The point is that monarchies and empires divided Europe in earlier millennia along a north/south axis that eerily corresponds to the insider/outsider divisions that would mark the later era. The footprint of Charlemagne's empire in the ninth century fits uncannily over the map of the original post-World War II "Europe"— the "Europe of Six" (France, West Germany, the Benelux countries of Belgium, Luxemburg, and the Netherlands, and Italy) that comprised the European Economic Community. Moreover, the divisions that defined the borders between historic empires find contemporary expression in the still potent religious divides between Roman Christianity, Orthodox Christianity, and Islam.[11]

The enlargement of the European Union eastward to include the Baltic states of Latvia, Lithuania, and Slovakia signaled the incorporation of Orthodox Christianity within "Europe." The process was made possible with the dissolution of the Soviet Union, and it was made palatable to the dominant Western European powers by explicit strategic decisions made by these Baltic states. States that had historically been at the crossroads of Europe and Russia chose decisively to tilt westward. "The 'clash of civilizations' echoed in the region as Balts strove to pull away from the East and join the West," observed Walter C. Clemens. "Nearly every Baltic government after 1991 looked west and north for trade and security."[12]

The recognition of Islam as a western religion has proved more difficult, as Islam has replaced Communism, in the eyes of many elites, activists, and ordinary citizens of the European Union, as the primary threat to Western civilization:

The 'Clash of Civilizations' theory, with its emphasis on cultural conflicts, combines well with the forms of nationalism promoted by such far-right politicians as Jean-Marie Le Pen and his Front National in France, the new

Right in England, and the Scandinavian anti-immigrant activists. The conception of a 'Muslim invasion' is widely held and promoted.[13]

The names of the xenophobic parties and leaders have changed and the success of these parties ebb and flow. But a great many Europeans remain preoccupied with high unemployment. They remain preoccupied, as well, with insecurities about national identity, they are impatient with the apparent ineptitude of governments, and frustrated with multi-level government. In the context of multi-level insecurities endemic to this era of European integration and globalization, the temptation to blame the "other" for political advantage has proven irresistible. Right-wing populist anti-immigrant parties, wasting few opportunities to exploit these insecurities, have gained electoral strength by manipulating these fears and blaming society's ills on immigrants. Because of their success, even center-left or traditional right parties have followed suit, and exclusionary policies on refugees, asylum and immigration with implicit anti-Islamic overtones have found their way onto the European Union agenda.

Thus, advancing a fortress Europe mentality at the EU summit in Seville in June 2002, British Prime Minister Tony Blair and his Spanish counterpart, José María Aznar, led a campaign to harden trade policy and suspend foreign aid to developing countries that refuse to take back refugees whose applications for asylum have been rejected. The plan was turned down by the summit amidst recriminations from immigrant and human rights groups, European allies (the Swedish prime minister called the proposal "stupid, unworkable and an historic mistake"), and even a rebuke directed at Blair from his own minister for development, Clare Short (who called the proposal "morally repugnant.")[14]

Even the French President, Jacques Chirac, who has made a career of outmaneuvering the far right on immigration issues, opposed any conditionality on aid insisting, "You are not going to solve problems by brandishing a sword, especially a wooden one." This, from the man who subsequently (in December 2003) inspired a passionate and often anguished debate across Europe about ethnic identity and inclusion when he endorsed the proposal from a presidential commission that would ban the wearing of "ostensibly religious" symbols in schools.

The new law, which according to polls received support from more than two-thirds of French citizens, was intended to affirm France's tradition of secular education as a source of social cohesion and was written to apply equally to Islamic headscarves, Jewish yarmulkes and large Christian crosses. Against the backdrop of French "Islamophobia" and decades of debate and zigzags in policy about the right of Islamic schoolgirls to wear veils or headscarves to public elementary and high schools, there was no mistaking the group targeted by the commission's proposal. "Certain religious signs, among them the Islamic veil, are multiplying in our schools," the French prime minister, Jean-Marie Raffarin, told the National Assembly. "They are taking on a political meaning. Some want to know how far they can go. We are giving them a response today."[15] Recognizing the broader geopolitical ramifications, Foreign Minister Dominique de Villepin reportedly warned the cabinet that the draft law would hurt France's relationships with largely Muslim countries.

Meanwhile, Turkey, the overwhelmingly Muslim country that has sought membership in "Europe" since the very creation of the European Economic Community (EEC) in 1958, remained on the outside looking in as the 2004 enlargement expanded EU membership to 25. As eight Eastern and Central European countries as well as Cyprus and Malta gained admission, many in Turkey expressed concerns about prejudice and misunderstandings that have governed Turko-European relations for 150 years since the Ottoman era.[16]

To be sure, there are legitimate grounds for concern regarding Turkish accession to the EU, including the requirements of greater respect for human rights and a reduced role of the military in government. In addition Brussels would like very much to see more sustained economic growth as a bulwark against Turkish emigration. It is also true that a diplomatic solution to the impasse with Greece over Cyprus would help clear the path to Turkish admission and, at the same time, remove the cloud over the admission of Cyprus.§ As talks hosted by Secretary-General Kofi Annan with both parties intensified in early 2004, Turkey pressed hard for its Cypriot compatriots to cut a deal. In February, with Ankara, Athens, London, and Washington pressing for a resolution, both Turkish and Greek Cypriot leaders accepted the "Annan plan"—which would give the Secretary-General the final authority to resolve any differences on reunification in advance of May 1, the date marking the accession of Cyprus to the European Union. Unfortunately, while Turkey strenuously backed the United Nations efforts at reunification and Turkish Cypriots voted for the UN Plan, Greek Cypriot leaders campaigned against the UN blueprint—and it was overwhelmingly rejected in a referendum. Hence, despite Turkish and Turkish Cypriot support for the UN and EU goal of bringing unity to Cyprus—and the opposing position from Greek Cypriots—in the absence of a unified Cyprus, only the Greek Cypriots got to join the EU (albeit amid controversy and threats of recriminations) on May 1, 2004. In appreciation of their support, the EU quickly rewarded the Turkish Cypriots with a set of measures to reduce their economic isolation, but the bigger issue of Turkish admission to Europe was left unresolved.

---

§Cyprus has been divided between Turkish Cypriots in the northern third of the island backed by Turkish troops and Greek Cypriots on the remainder of the island since a sequence of events in 1974 that included ethnic violence, a coup in Nicosia promulgated by the military regime in Greece, the rapid introduction of Turkish troops into the north, and the introduction of a UN peacekeeping force to keep order. Although Turkish Cypriots have declared an independent state, only Turkey recognizes them. The United Nations has sponsored interminable rounds of talks in the interim, as peacekeepers remained stationed on the island since 1964. See: Adamantia Polis, "Cyprus," in Joel Krieger, ed. The Oxford Companion to Politics of the World, 2nd ed. (New York: Oxford University Press, 2001), p. 189.

Against this backdrop, many Turks resent the appearance of double standards. Why, they wonder, should Turkey be held back but Cyprus as well as a host of eastern and central European countries, which have their own problems with human rights and democratic transitions, be invited to join the EU? Why was Turkey kept unceremoniously waiting in candidate status for 15 years before the start of formal negotiations on the country's application for full membership? Why was Turkey kept in limbo, as a candidate member but off the accession list and with no commitment to begin negotiations, despite Ankara's very strong backing from Washington, including a personal telephone call to the EU president on the eve of the decision by President Bush, who was looking to bring Turkey on Iraq's northern border firmly into the fold for the anticipated war?[17]

Not unreasonably, many Turks think the country's Muslim identity and its population (at 70 million, it would be second only to Germany in the EU) are the real reasons for its lengthy delay in gaining admission to Europe. They will not soon forget the stark and remarkably undiplomatic declaration issued by the former French president Valéry Giscard d'Estaing in November 2002, one month before the EU decided at the Copenhagen summit not to include Turkey in their expansion list. "[Turkey's] capital is not in Europe," asserted Giscard. "[It has] a different culture, a different approach, and a different way of life. It is not a European country."[18]

His counterpart, former West German Chancellor Helmut Schmidt, was equally dismissive about Turkey's role in Europe and even more transparent about the underlying cultural and religious concern that motivated the exclusion. Turkey's admission "would open the door for similarly plausible full membership of other Muslim nations in Africa and in the Middle East," observed Schmidt. "That could result in the political union degenerating into nothing more than a free trade community."[19] It was not Giscard's language that made his remark an instant headline throughout Europe and the cause of much acrimony in Turkey, although his language was dramatic, asserting that Turkish membership would result in "the end of Europe." Rather it was his position as chairman of the Convention on the Future of Europe—his authority as the person in charge of the project of drafting a constitution for a United Europe—that made his declaration about Turkey sound a lot like a gavel silencing Turkey's aspirations.

More salt was rubbed into the Turkish wound in April 2004. French President Jacques Chirac's ruling party said it opposed Turkey holding talks about accession with the European Union before the end of the year and Alain Juppé, a former prime minister and influential Chirac advisor, said countries on the periphery of the growing EU, such as Turkey, "have no business joining (the bloc) otherwise it will be diluted."[20]

The historic decision by the European Commission is October 2004 to recommend that the EU begin membership talks with Turkey speaks to important changes both in Turkey and in the EU. But many challenges lie ahead for a geographically and culturally expanded EU before we can conclude that the clash of civilizations in Europe has been resolved.

The Clash between Europe and the United States

The divisions between the United States and Europe also cut deep. The worryingly rancorous relations between allies and friends run deeper than the wounds over Iraq, which had begun to heal by spring 2003. "A year ago, at the Davos World Economic Forum, I saw elephants fly," as Thomas Friedman put it, using his unique gift for metaphor to emphasize the strange gravity-defying claims that were floated in January 2003, as the United States and Europe battled diplomatically during the prelude to war in Iraq. "At this year's Davos forum, though, all the elephants came crashing down. Turns out elephants can't fly after all—and the world is a better place for it."[21]

In other words, the United States had come to recognize in the intervening year that it could make war but not execute regime change, rebuild Iraq, and secure an effective transition to democracy without the assistance of the United Nations as well as that of major allies such as France and Germany. Similarly, France had come to realize that it could not "galvanize anti-U.S. sentiment to make itself the great global Uncola to America's Coca-Cola . . . [and] make France the supreme power in Europe, marginalizing Britain."[22]

In fact, rather than pulling off a win-win, France lost on several fronts. France and its allies couldn't stop the war; France was left poorly positioned to shape the post-war order in Iraq or benefit materially from the rebuilding; and, its hand was weakened when it came to shaping the map of the Middle East. In addition, and perhaps most significantly in the long run, France's anti-U.S. posture and inflexibility at the UN drove countries such as Poland and Spain more deeper into the U.S. camp and appears to have sparked the determination of the new members from East-Central Europe to try to break the Franco-German hammerlock on EU affairs. Then, the surprising election of José Luis Rodríguez Zapatero as Spanish prime minister in the aftermath of the Madrid bombings in March 2004 shifted the valance of Spain's role vis-à-vis EU politics, the United States, and the war in Iraq.

As Zapatero quickly announced the demobilization of Spanish troops in Iraq, the debate about the meaning of the election continued: was it pay back to Aznar for leading Spain into a war opposed by the vast majority of Spanish citizens and misleading them about the sources of terror (initially blaming Basque separatists)? Or was the decision to withdraw appeasement to terror—and an ominous sign that terrorism directed at an uneasy European electorate would benefit Al Qaeda and its associated networks? However that debate played out, the dramatic reversal in Spanish policy—followed by Poland's declaration in August 2004 that it would pull its troops out of Iraq—underscored both the force of European divisions over Iraq and the volatility of policy directions.

From the European perspective, the divisions over the war in Iraq built on the resentments of America's powerful allies who are not quite powerful enough—or sufficiently cohesive and strategic—to counter-balance a United States that appears willing to throw off the self-imposed strategic restraint that characterized its geopolitical stance in the Atlantic Alliance for a half-century. France and Britain are poised to launch a potentially significant cooperative defense initiative: a set of highly trained rapid-deployment units that are designed to operate effectively (although not exclusively) under a UN mandate. The initiative is intended to beef up the EU's capacity for Europe's defense as well as its ability for humanitarian intervention.

As many have observed, the glaring deficiencies in European military capabilities that were revealed in Bosnia and Kosovo and which forced Europeans to rely on America for military muscle placed a big new idea on the EU agenda: the need for a technologically sophisticated and organizationally effective military capability as part of a far more robust common foreign and security policy (CFSP). The security challenges of the post-9/11 era, the divisions within Europe over the war in Iraq, and the dramatic enlargement of the EU have complicated the project of forging a coherent and effective European geopolitical strategy. But clearly the time has come and the political will is building.

However effectively the CFSP agenda of the European Union advances in the years ahead, nothing is likely to reduce the power asymmetry between Europe and the United States very significantly. Yet even a fairly modest increase in European capacity to intervene independently and with good effect to promote regional stability or prevent humanitarian catastrophes in failed states might have important geopolitical multiplier effects. As with the steel tariffs, where Europe was able to exert sufficient influence through the WTO to stare down U.S. protectionist measures and force an American president to blink first, even small doses of European resolve and cohesion might provoke an effort to recalibrate U.S./E.U. relations. Steady movement by the EU and its most powerful member states to strengthen both the capacity and the cohesion of European-based regional defense might encourage an American president to think twice about throwing off the mantle of self-imposed restraints that provided an effective check against unilateralist stirrings. For the foreseeable future, the United States seems destined to preserve its asymmetrical power vis-à-vis the Europeans, but to what end?

"[T]he only stable and successful international order Americans can imagine is one that has the United States at its center," observes Robert Kagan in his influential book, *Of Paradise and Power: America and Europe in the New World Order*.[23] "Nor can the Americans conceive of an international order that is not defended by power, and specifically American power."[24] Kagan is right on this point—at least for now with the muscular approach to power inaugurated by the Bush Doctrine holding sway—but the consequences are profound.

America's assertions of hegemonic right on the world stage drive a wedge through the Atlantic Alliance, and this is especially true because Europeans know instinctively and by the decades long experience of European integration that the autonomous exercise of power is illusory and the effects fleeting. This recognition, however, is not mainly driven by the disparity of power or the psychology of weakness or the international idealism described by Robert Kagan. There is much to learn from Kagan's influential essay on European/American relations, but he misses the critical point when he writes, "Rather than viewing the United States as a Gulliver tied down by Lilliputian threads, American leaders should realize that they are hardly constrained at all, that Europe is not really capable of constraining the United States."[25]

True, the United States is not significantly restrained by European power or even by their different strategic perspectives on the use of power and their greater reluctance to use military force. But the more important observation about European/American relations is that these "Lilliputian threads" are pulling the United States, however reluctantly, in the direction it needs to go. Sovereignty is not sacrosanct; politics is compromise; global governance is multi-level and multilateral, not by choice or ideological preference, but of necessity. America should stop treating allies in Europe like six-inch inhabitants of remote nations and reflect on their claims. It should free itself from the mentality about strategic power that sees only brute force and the threat of force as the guarantor of the international order. It should move past the mindset (shared by Kagan) that views the European alternatives of diplomacy, appeals to international law, and consensus-driven policy as little more than unseemly squeamishness about the use of force. Both Kagan and American policy makers dismiss or ignore these geopolitical realities exhibited in the European Union and thus far better understood by Europeans.

Hence, it is not the actual exercise of state power so much as the perspectives on state power and the use of force to advance interests that most decisively divide Europe and the United States. I would add that divisions of this kind—regarding beliefs about the proper place of compromise and diplomacy, the morality of war to advance geopolitical interests, and what Kagan calls "a set of ideals and principles regarding the utility and morality of power"[26]—express a very significant and politically potent trans-Atlantic clash of civilizations. As the *Sturm und Drang* between the United States and Europe over Iraq begins to fade, the underlying tensions in political cultures, respect for international law and the sanctity and utility of treaty obligations, and in elemental visions of both the global order and domestic politics and society surface with greater clarity.

Far more than disagreements over Iraq, the United States and Europe are divided—and are likely to remain divided—over values and domestic political agendas, geopolitical and economic conflicts of interest, and resentments that will inevitably bubble to the surface as a consequence of the asymmetries of power between Europe and the United States.

Making the most of its prestige and unrivaled power and influence, the United States came to regard international treaties and conventions as a threat to sovereignty and America's capacity to control the terms of globalization. Hence the United States has failed to ratify treaties or recognize conventions held dear to Europeans on banning land mines and biological weapons, the establishment of the International Criminal Court, the Kyoto Protocol on global warming, and the Comprehensive Test Ban Treaty (CBTB). In December 2001 it abrogated the ABM Treaty.

European and American perspectives differ on the response to crime (Europeans are overwhelming opposed to capital punishment). Perspectives differ on climate change (Europeans are far more willing to work aggressively to reduce energy use and limit greenhouse gas emissions to mitigate climate change). Perspectives differ on arms control (all 25 current EU members have ratified the CBTB while the United States boycotted a September 2003 conference on facilitating ratification and appears to be trying to kill it).

Thus U.S./European divisions run deep on key global policies that tap deeply held convictions and values—and disclose crucial disagreements about the role, function, and significance of international law, treaties, and conventions. European governments are far more inclined to see all these instruments of international civil society as ways to maximize state power by pooling state power. Washington doesn't want to be pinned down by Lilliputians.

In a way that political leaders in the United States don't seem to recognize, divisions over convictions and values (soft power) can have grave consequences on America's capacity to recruit allies for war (hard power).[27] Europeans are far less likely to join the United States in Iraq or accept American dictates about the war on terrorism when the United States refuses to participate in a coalition to combat global climate change through the Kyoto Protocol.

This internecine clash of civilizations flares up with every assertion by an American leader (and these are very commonplace) that the United States holds a monopoly on "Western values" and morality and can alone define their just and appropriate application around the world. President Bush's statement in his rare prime time news conference in April 2004 to defend his Iraq policy did not play well in Europe: "Now is the time, and Iraq is the place, in which the enemies of the civilized world are testing the will of the civilized world. We must not waver."[28] As one European journalist observed, "an increasing number of commentators believe that [Europe and the United States] are divided not just by interests but by values, which suggests a deeper rift than occasional differences of interests."[29]

Many Europeans are put off by any claims that the United States knows the one best way to organize society (one that accepts a level of poverty, inequality, and social marginalization with racial overtones that most Europeans find repugnant). As Europe becomes increasingly secular, the incessant public affirmations of faith among American politicians and office seekers and the increasingly transparent use of religion to create wedge issues—around gay marriage or abortion rights for example—provides yet another touchstone of transatlantic distinctions over values and the proper conduct of politics and public policy.

"What Europeans find perturbing about America . . . is precisely what most Americans believe to be their nation's strongest suit: its unique mix of moralistic religiosity, minimal provision for public welfare, and maximal market freedom— the 'American way of life'—coupled with a missionary foreign policy ostensibly directed at exporting that same cluster of values and practices," observes Tony Judt, explaining how deep rooted the growing differences in values and priorities between Europeans and Americans have become. He went on to add, "Here the U.S. is ill served by globalization, which highlights for the world's poorer countries the costs of exposure to economic competition and reminds West Europeans, after the long sleep of the cold war, of the true fault lines bisecting the hitherto undifferentiated 'West.' "[30]

Clearly, Iraq was just the tip of a large iceberg when it comes to the deep divisions that roil transatlantic relations and cloud perceptions among allies. In Chapter 5 we will revisit the implications of Western disunity for the prospects of collective security and the shape of geopolitics in the contemporary post-9/11 global order. For now, we turn to a very pressing set of questions. Can Europe be Europe? Or, pressured by the hegemonic dictates of American foreign policy and squeezed by the competitive pressures of globalization, will Europe lose its distinctiveness and become something it never wished to become: a more pliable one-shape-fits-all outpost of American global branding?

GLOBALIZATION AND
THE EUROPEAN MODEL

Country by country across "old Europe" the ensemble of political-cultural values and defining economic and social policy that comprise a European model can be viewed as variations on a theme. Countries differ in important ways, but each country's cultural and political life is anchored by a broad consensus about bedrock values and policies: a European economic and social model that is very different from its U.S. counterpart. For some three decades after the Second World War, across Western Europe a tacit alliance between the organized working class and large-scale business anchored a set of nationally specific "postwar settlements" which set the framework for a general understanding of European party competition, political economy, and public policy.

States intervened extensively to regulate economies, promote economic growth, and secure nearly full employment while expanding welfare provision. Within this model associated with European social democracy, Keynesian economics provided the rationale for a vigorous, activist governmental stance to assure aggregate demand through high levels of spending that would in turn stimulate economic growth.

As a result, the harmonious, positive-sum politics of class compromise became crystallized in the tacit agreements of the postwar settlement, and a period of sustained growth replaced traditional zero-sum conflict. On one end of the spectrum of variants, the model includes—one might say embraces—the most robust case, Swedish social democracy. In the Swedish case, the electoral strength of the Social Democratic Party (SAP) combined with the favored status and influence enjoyed by trade unions, led to a vast array of comprehensive, egalitarian, redistributive, and universal welfare provisions. On the other pole, one finds the far more minimalist "Labourism" that serves as the dramatic foil for Tony Blair's New Labour agenda. It was weaker in its institutional reach (the National Economic Development Council was no Commissariat Général du Plan) and less robust in its policy aims (no serious consideration was given to worker participation as in German codetermination or works councils, and never even a hint of collective share ownership through the build up of wage earner funds as in Sweden's Meidner Plan).

The oil crises of 1973 and 1979, like lightening bolts from the global economy, demonstrated the down side of interdependence long before the concept "globalization" was introduced. The worldwide economic slump they triggered posed a tremendous challenge to the European model, which relied on high growth to sustain high social expenditures. The oil shock inspired a backlash against welfare states and social protections that ushered in the decade of the 1980s symbolized by the rise to power of Ronald Reagan in the United States and Margaret Thatcher in the United Kingdom. The downturn in domestic economies that created havoc for governments across Europe and sent governing models skittering in different directions had significant regional implications. The hard economic and political times temporally stalled the progress toward European integration. Hard times delayed and complicated the movement toward economic and monetary union that would lead ultimately to the adoption of a single currency by eleven EU countries in 1998 and the withdrawal of national currencies throughout the euro zone in 2002.

The 1990s, the decade in which globalization came into its own and one that witnessed a tremendous acceleration in European integration, were not kind to the European economic and social model. For a start, globalization tends to favor national systems like those of Britain and the United States, which rely more on private contractual and market-driven arrangements and less on state capacity and political bargaining to determine distributional outcomes. At the same time, global investment strategies ostracize markets such as Germany or the Scandinavian countries, which rely more on citizenship status, institutionalized bargaining and coordination, and state-sponsored arrangements. Globalization increases the mobility of capital and labor across borders, and expresses its deregulatory and anti-institutional bias in dramatic patterns of Foreign Direct Investment (FDI), which substantially favor Britain over Germany, for example.[31]

In this way, the processes of globalization tend to dissolve negotiated coordination between nationally based capital and labor, challenge progressive distributive bargains, and punish countries with more egalitarian policy legacies and institutional capacities. As a result, for political leaders who accept this framework, there was little alternative but to deregulate labor markets, reduce tax burdens, and roll back social protections, "else they suffer the wrath of profit-maximising investors and alienate voters."[32]

In this climate of opinion, the Maastricht Treaty (ratified in 1993) specified a set of "convergence criteria" to govern a country's entry into the euro zone. German demands that there be permanent mechanisms to strengthen both the single currency and fiscal discipline lead to the incorporation of a "stability and growth pact" in the Amsterdam Treaty of 1997.[33] To put it bluntly, the macroeconomic and social policy orientations mandated by the EMU convergence criteria—deficits below 3 percent of Gross Domestic Product (GDP), inflation rates no more than 1.5 percent greater than the average of the three members with the lowest rates, and so forth—play havoc with the postwar settlement distributional bargains that underlie social democratic politics and sustain the European economic and social model. In light of competitive pressures and various county-by-country constituency demands, something had to give. But it was not the model that makes Europe still Europe, which remains battered, criticized, modified, but unbowed. As we'll see below, when Europe's social model and the demands of domestic politics ran up against the dictates of the stability and growth pact, it was the pact—a hugely important symbol of collective will and fiscal rectitude—that was left in tatters.

The European Model: Variations on a Theme

Will Hutton provides a useful summary of what the model looks like today and its distinctiveness from what citizens expect and tolerate in the United States:

> [E]ach European economic and social model is characterized by a combination of income redistribution, social insurance, means-tested social benefits, and provision of public health and education that makes taxes and social security contributions higher than in the United States—and a combination of employment protection, labor market regulation, and higher trade union representation that buttresses the rights and powers of Europe's workers more than those of their counterparts in the United States. . . . [T]hese mechanisms do not create unemployment, nor have they damaged Europe's powerful record on enterprise and productivity. What they have done is to produce an array of social outcomes which on every important measure are significantly better than in the United States.[34]

Hutton's conclusion may seem implausible to many Americans, but most Europeans would applaud it instinctively. What policies are deemed better, after all, hinges less on the results of arcane debates about the sources of job creation or loss or the most effective measures of competitiveness, and more on convictions about what should be valued most in society.

That said, Europe can only be Europe in the sense Hutton identifies the distinctiveness of the European model of society if EU countries—led by Germany, France, and the U.K.—can sustain robust and competitive economies that can withstand the downsizing pressures of global competition and challenge the common American wisdom that all successful economies look very much like Thomas Friedman describes and the "Washington Consensus" prescribes.

What distinguishes each of the EU's three dominant economies, and each of their social and economic models from each other? The German model has sometimes been called a "high-everything" model or more seriously a "social market economy" that combines a free market economy with a sizeable layer of social benefits (such as savings subsidies and a comprehensive vocational training system) that are intended less to serve as transfer payments and more to produce dividends for German competitiveness.[35] The model relies on a highly skilled and trained, highly paid work force locked into a social contract that results in a "high-welfare nation."[36] Despite the challenges associated with the high costs of production and recalcitrant unions, the model has sustained for Germany in the period since the oil crisis of 1973 a more competitive global position than that of most competitors. At its best, the "combination of high skills, high investment, and commitment to long-term organic business growth is at the heart of the German productivity miracle, endowing the German economy with its capacity to build companies, large and small, that are extraordinarily adept at diversifying and upgrading production while maintaining high quality."[37]

From a British or American perspective, however, Germany has gone from the "strong man" to the "sick man" of Europe. Economic growth has stagnated and unemployment is high at over 10 percent. To critics of the German model who view it as outmoded in this era of globalization and the race to the bottom to reduce labor costs, Chancellor Gerhard Schröder's tax cuts and his reform package passed by the Bundestag just before Christmas 2003—his Agenda 2010 that is intended to deregulate labor markets and reduce social expenditures—are too little, too late.

For these critics, the U.K. represents the European social and economic model that is best suited to competitive advantage in the global economy, one that is a European outlier located somewhere between the American laissez-faire approach and the European social and economic model. Britain thus plays a particular role within the European and international economy, one that has been reinforced by international competitive pressures in this global age. From the mid-1980s onward, the single market initiative of the EU has attracted foreign investment by according insider status to non-EU-based companies, so long as minimum local content requirements are met. Due to such factors as low costs, a business friendly political climate, government-sponsored incentives, weak unions, and a large pool of potential nonunionized recruits, the United Kingdom is by far the favored location in Europe for FDI.

For U.K. governments from Thatcher to Blair, FDI has proven a congenial market-driven alternative to state intervention as a means to improve competitiveness, expose U.K. producers to "lean production" techniques and managerial strategies that reinforced government designs to weaken unions, establish an enabling partnership with business, and achieve competitiveness on the basis of reliability, enhanced skills, the quality of products, and the capacity for innovation. In recent years, the U.K. has grown twice as fast as Germany and experiences far lower unemployment. On the negative side, however, the British model encompasses far greater inequality than its "great power" counterparts, and relies on a system of production that proliferates nonstandard and insecure jobs without traditional social protections, a growing sector in which women and ethnic minorities are significantly overrepresented. As a result, within the EU-15, Britain has assumed a specialized profile as a producer of relatively low-technology, low-value-added products made by a comparatively low-paid, segmented, weakly organized, and easily dismissed labor force.[38]

Each in a distinctive fashion, Germany and the U.K. eagerly embraced globalization, but not so in France. With its traditional commitment to *dirigisme* (a leading role for the state in the management of economic affairs) as the touchstone of its economic model, the liberalization of the French economy does not come easy. In addition, France's social model is anchored in profound commitments to public health and state-sponsored education that rival the much-vaunted Scandinavian model, against a backdrop of highly partisan, easily mobilized, and adversarial labor-management relations that resonate with that of Southern Europe.[39]

Critics looking at France see excessive social protection, an overbearing state impeding market-based adjustments and subduing the entrepreneurial culture, and little enthusiasm among political or economic elites for economic liberalism. When people think of France and globalization they are still inclined to think first of the high-visibility antiglobalization agitprop of José Bové. In August 1999, the previously obscure sheep farmer led an assault on a McDonald's restaurant in Southern France to protest U.S. retaliatory trade sanctions against France. Then, Bové managed to smuggle enormous chunks of Roquefort cheese into Seattle in November 1999, where he helped lead the legendary protests at the WTO summit, thereby securing his worldwide fame and cementing the identification of the French countryside with the antiglobalization movement.[40]

Next, when people think of the French response to globalization, they probably think of the rather implausible intensification of workplace and labor market regulation through the *Réduction du temps de travail* (RTT)—the policy first announced in the Socialist's electoral platform in 1997 to reduce by law the number of hours worked per week from 39 to 35, with no corresponding reduction in pay.* The policy was intended to spur job creation (through recombination) and competitiveness, but in the wider context of economic liberalization which emphasizes the signal importance of managerial flexibility, the French decision to mandate reductions in the workweek seems anachronistic at best.

For the French, however, it represents taking both globalization and traditional social protections seriously. The RTT, which only requires an average of 35 hours, has resulted in increased managerial flexibility to meet cyclical demand.[41] In addition, resentments have grown among employees as employers have pressed for wage restraints in return for the reduced workweek. A survey published in September 2003 revealed that 36 percent of respondents would prefer to see a return to the 39-hour week and another 18 percent would like to see the RTT temporarily suspended. In addition, fully two-thirds of the respondents considered the 35-hour week an ineffective measure against rising unemployment. What is more, big employers have used the RTT to cut social security contributions and impose new working methods.[42] Then, in July 2004, 98 percent of the French workers at a car components factory near Lyons owned by Bosch, a German automotive conglomerate, voted to accede to company demands to accept a longer working week. A sign of the times (and the first such vote in France) the decision might encourage movement toward a gradual de-facto unraveling of the 35-hour week in France. If so, rather than bucking the trend toward an expanded work week, which is being pressed aggressively by leading companies in Germany, France might actually contribute to the broader European trend toward longer hours and greater managerial flexibility. Perhaps the unintended consequences of this radical socialist reform provide just the proof that is needed to demonstrate that one way or another—as Gordon and Meunier put it via "globalization by stealth"[43]—France has been gradually adjusting to global competitive pressures and weaning itself off its *dirigiste* traditions.

In fact knowledgeable observers insist that France has enhanced competitiveness and adapted to globalization quite dramatically in the last two decades. "[T]he real story of the French economy of the past twenty years is not so much how the state has maintained its traditional grip, but rather how the country has gradually, and quietly, adapted to the requirements of the emerging global, liberal economy," observe Gordon and Meunier. ". . . Indeed, by any measure—

---

*The 35-hour week came into effect on January 1, 2000, for businesses with more than 20 employees and on January 1, 2002, for businesses with 20 employees or less, with overtime payments mandated for those who worked longer hours. This legislation was then watered down in 2003, permitting firms to extend the work week to 39 hours (or more) in return for negotiated wage increases.

privatization, the role of the stock market, the globalization of French industry, openness to trade, exchange rate policy, taxation, labor relations, or adoption of technology—it is apparent that France has steadily, if reluctantly, liberalized its economy and opened it up to international competition and influence."[44] How well has the French "new economy" adapted to the competitive pressures of globalization?

Reviewing the "Big 3" of Europe we see three significant variations on the theme of a European economic and social model. In an important sense, as they go, so goes Europe. Do they have what it takes to sustain the competitive edge they need to keep the European social and economic model afloat?

Europe's Big Three in the Global Economy

There is no denying that the Global Profiles of Germany, France and the United Kingdom identify highly integrated and very influential global players. Although the number of national missions abroad is but an imprecise measure of international political influence and integration, it is notable that the United Kingdom has a greater number of missions abroad (188) than does the United States (142) and that the number of foreign diplomatic missions in France (150) nearly matches that of the United States (153). As former colonial powers, which retain significant ties and influence throughout the world, and as members of the P-5 (permanent members of the UN Security Council), the most select diplomatic club in the world, the full geopolitical integration of Britain and France in global affairs is guaranteed.

When it comes to economic integration, Germany's Global Profile begins to reveal the true measure of its significance in the global economy. With the exports of goods and services accounting for fully one-third of its GDP and the imports of goods and services accounting for nearly 30 percent of its GDP, it is clear that Germany exhibits very substantial economic integration. With the largest economy in Europe and such a high degree of global economic integration, it seems reasonable, in fact, to consider Germany the regional economic hegemon and to anticipate very considerable influence in EU policy debates.

Few doubt that Germany, France, and the United Kingdom each enjoy considerable global influence well beyond Europe or that they are the "great powers" in EU Europe (although as we will see, other EU countries have come to resent their growing assertion of power and influence). In this section, we focus on their competitive capabilities. As we argued in Chapter 2 with reference to the United States, the competitiveness that matters most for cutting-edge economies is the competitiveness that is critically linked to the capacity for rapid innovation measured by global market share.

Following Michael Storper and Robert Salais, we can identify three groups of products for which global competition for market share is very likely to be linked to product quality (including innovative design and differentiation)

FIGURE 3.1
France Global Profile

Economic Integration	Political Integration
France — bar chart, %GDP: Exports of Goods and Services as % of GDP (2000) 28.66; Imports of Goods and Services as % of GDP (2000) 23.63; Foreign Direct Investment (2000) 3.34	Number of diplomatic missions in France 150 Number of French diplomatic mission abroad 105 • Joined the United Nations in 1945. • Ratified Kyoto Protocol May 31, 2002. • Ratified the Convention on the Elimination of All Forms of Discrimination against Women on December 14, 1983.
Information Flows International mail (letters per person per year sent or received from abroad) 1997 15 International phone calls (outgoing minutes per person per year) 1997 58	**Cultural Influences** Percentage of population foreign born (1990–1995) 10.4% Imported feature films as percentage of total films distributed (1994–1998) 56%
People Flows Number of students abroad/number of foreign students (thousand) 1994-1997: French students abroad 39.2 thousand Foreign students in France 138.2 thousand	**Security and Military Interaction** Military expenditure as percentage of government spending 5.9 Arms exports (percentage of total exports) 1 Arms imports (percentage of total imports) 0.3

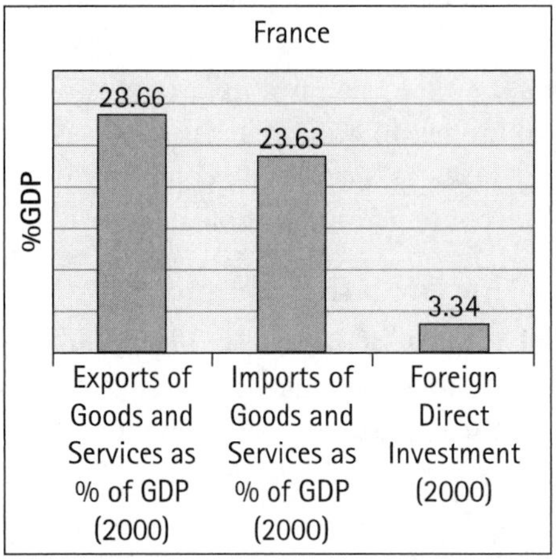

FIGURE 3.2
U.K. Global Profile

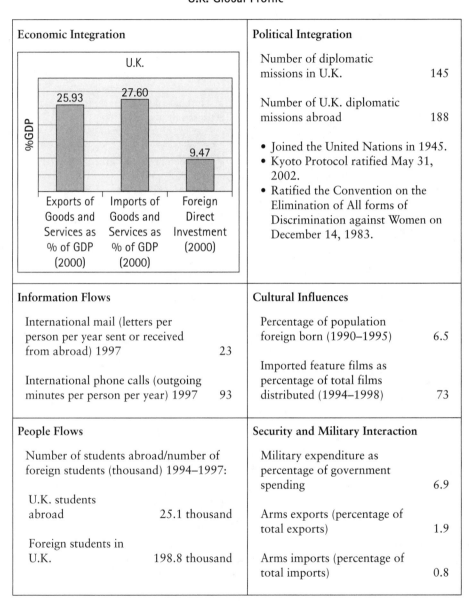

Economic Integration	Political Integration
U.K. (bar chart, %GDP) Exports of Goods and Services as % of GDP (2000): 25.93 Imports of Goods and Services as % of GDP (2000): 27.60 Foreign Direct Investment (2000): 9.47	Number of diplomatic missions in U.K. — 145 Number of U.K. diplomatic missions abroad — 188 • Joined the United Nations in 1945. • Kyoto Protocol ratified May 31, 2002. • Ratified the Convention on the Elimination of All forms of Discrimination against Women on December 14, 1983.
Information Flows International mail (letters per person per year sent or received from abroad) 1997 — 23 International phone calls (outgoing minutes per person per year) 1997 — 93	**Cultural Influences** Percentage of population foreign born (1990–1995) — 6.5 Imported feature films as percentage of total films distributed (1994–1998) — 73
People Flows Number of students abroad/number of foreign students (thousand) 1994–1997: U.K. students abroad — 25.1 thousand Foreign students in U.K. — 198.8 thousand	**Security and Military Interaction** Military expenditure as percentage of government spending — 6.9 Arms exports (percentage of total exports) — 1.9 Arms imports (percentage of total imports) — 0.8

FIGURE 3.3
Germany Global Profile

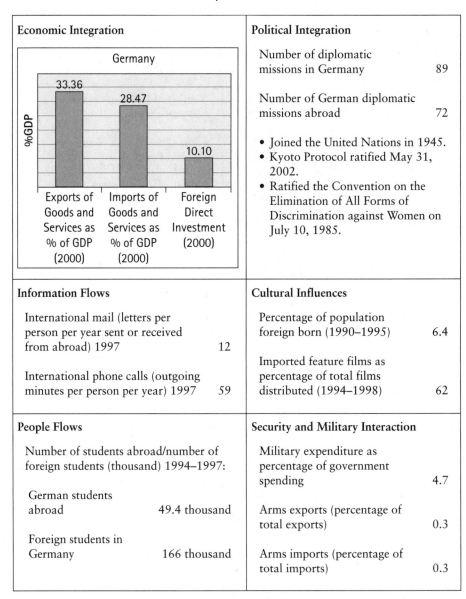

Economic Integration

Germany

Political Integration

Number of diplomatic
missions in Germany   89

Number of German diplomatic
missions abroad   72

- Joined the United Nations in 1945.
- Kyoto Protocol ratified May 31, 2002.
- Ratified the Convention on the Elimination of All Forms of Discrimination against Women on July 10, 1985.

Information Flows

International mail (letters per
person per year sent or received
from abroad) 1997   12

International phone calls (outgoing
minutes per person per year) 1997 59

Cultural Influences

Percentage of population
foreign born (1990–1995)   6.4

Imported feature films as
percentage of total films
distributed (1994–1998)   62

People Flows

Number of students abroad/number of
foreign students (thousand) 1994–1997:

German students
abroad   49.4 thousand

Foreign students in
Germany   166 thousand

Security and Military Interaction

Military expenditure as
percentage of government
spending   4.7

Arms exports (percentage of
total exports)   0.3

Arms imports (percentage of
total imports)   0.3

and cutting-edge technological innovations rather than to simple price-competitiveness.[45] The first cluster includes science-based high technology industries or HTI (e.g. chemicals, pharmaceuticals, engines, telecommunications equipment, aircraft, analyzing and controlling equipment). The second group consists of design-intensive or craft-based products or DIC (such as clothing, fashion products, furniture, watches and clocks, musical instruments). The third cluster is comprised of machine tools and precision metalworking machinery (PNM), a classic indicator of competitive strength in primary industrial applications scattered across the economy, which require technological prowess, and rapid cycles of innovation.[46]

See Table 3.1 for a very compact comparative summary of U.K., German, and French competitiveness from 1992 to 2000 (the last year for which comprehensive data is available), analyzed by reference to technological mastery and product quality in these key sectors as indicated by the composition of trade and international market share.

The high-technology (HTI) cluster accounts for one-quarter of U.K. total exports and the U.K. exports in this sector represent 5.3 percent of world exports in the 1993–2000 period. Also on the positive side, the value of exports outpaced imports by $5 billion. Within HTI, the U.K. is extremely strong in telecommunications equipment, which has enjoyed a steady rate of growth in exports annually between 1996 and 2000, placing second behind the United States in its exports, slightly ahead of Japan, and 15 percent above Germany (which would come as a big surprise to many!). With regard to the design-intensive sector (DCI) and the machine tools and precision metalworking sector (PNM) there is little to suggest comparative specialization or advantage. The U.K. performs well (or moderately well) in a few branches within each cluster, but does not appear to be specialized in a way that leverages its strengths across either sector.[47]

The competitive strengths of the U.K. economy are confirmed in some key benchmarks used in *The Global Competitiveness Report.* Especially noteworthy are the U.K.'s superiority in Microeconomic Competitiveness in which it achieved a first place ranking in all three components of National Business Environment and two "1s" and a "2" in the three measures of Company Operations and Strategy (for an overall ranking of 3). The U.K. ranked 11 in Growth Competitiveness. Hence, despite some competitive disadvantages associated with the U.K.'s market-driven model—national savings rate (68), government expenditure (55), government success in technology promotion (54)—the U.K. profile suggests a glass that may not be brimming over, but one that is certainly far more than half full.[48]

Whatever sluggishness and rigidities may be troubling the German economy, they are not revealed in the country's global market share and competitive advantage. Germany is impressive across all three sectors in which innovation and quality-competitiveness are the primary sources of comparative advantage.

TABLE 3.1

Comparative degree of specialization in high–technology, design–intensive/craft–based and precision machinery metalworking industries for U.K., Germany and France, averages 1993–2000

CLUSTERS	U.K.	GERMANY	FRANCE
High-technology industries			
Value of exports ($billion)	61.17	79.99	55.81
Value of imports ($billion)	56.11	64.91	44.23
Country's share of total world exports in cluster (%)	6.63%	8.72%	6.08%
Cluster's share of country's total exports (%)	25.01%	15.86%	20.22%
Design-intensive/craft-based industry			
Value of exports ($billion)	17.65	35.52	23.09
Value of imports ($billion)	23.45	33.91	21.41
Country's share of total world exports in cluster (%)	4.08%	8.26%	5.34%
Cluster's share of country's total exports (%)	7.36%	7.17%	8.07%
Precision machinery and metalworking			
Value of exports ($billion)	1.86	7.29	1.42
Value of imports ($billion)	1.85	3.16	2.09
Country's share of total world exports in cluster (%)	4.64%	18.43%	3.58%
Cluster's share of country's total exports (%)	0.77%	1.46%	0.52%

Source: SITC (Standard International Trade Classification) Rev.2 and Rev.3; our calculation.
Note: Clusters definition based on SITC's. High-technologies' SITCs Rev.2 = 524, 541, 713, 714, 751, 159, 759, 761, 762, 763, 764, 772, 776, 792, 871, 872, 874. Design-intensive/craft-based industry = 551, 553, 611, 612, 613, 651, 652, 653, 654, 655, 656, 657, 658, 659, 666, 665, 724, 821, 851, 881, 882, 883, 884, 885, 897, 898. Precision Machinery and metalworking = 696, 731, 733, 735, 737.

In fact, in each of the three sectors Germany achieved a greater share of total world exports than either of its major European competitors. Its well-known dominance in machine tools (at nearly one-fifth of the total world export market) is amply confirmed, as is its strength in high-technology industries (at nearly one-tenth the global export market). But who would have expected Germany (with roughly 8 percent of total world exports) to out-compete France (with just over

5 percent global export market share) in design-intensive and craft-based industry, which includes clothing, fashion, and furniture?

The Global Competitiveness Report confirms considerable strength, most notably in Microeconomic Competitiveness. Germany ranks first in Sophistication of Company Operations and Strategy and fourth in the overall Microeconomic Competitiveness Rank. The Growth Competitiveness Rank, although strong at 14, also reflects some substantial competitive disadvantages where you would expect to find them, especially in the World Economic Forum framework that is tilted in favor of market-driven rather than social market economies. The *Report* identifies weaknesses in several areas: in elements of the Macroeconomic Index such as Government Expenditure (71); in aspects of the National Business Environment such as distortive subsidies (71); and in other indicators such as wage flexibility (79) and hiring and firing practices (79). Germany's impressive success in the quality-competitive high-tech industry clusters we reviewed does not come by accident, but it does come within a particular economic and social model that is difficult to sustain in a global economy that privileges economic liberalism.

France's performance in the global economy—measured both by its global export market share in quality-competitive high-tech clusters and in the balance sheet provided by *The Global Competitiveness Report*—provides some answers and raises some questions about its competitiveness. For example, the high-technology cluster provides one-fifth of the country's total exports, but ranks below both Germany and the U.K. in its share of total world exports. This mixed record reflects a relatively narrow scope in technology industries. France tends to be weakly represented in microelectronics and other core technologies, which are dominated by foreign firms, and to be specialized predominantly in systems engineering and large-scale applied technology systems such as those used in aircraft and space hardware and in large communications systems.[49]

High-quality and narrow specialization results in successful high-technology *filières* (commodity production chains) but fairly limited global market share. This pattern reflects the statist tilt of the French economic model, which privileges firms that benefit from state financing and purchasing that is typical of large scale technology systems. In the DIC sector, as in the high-technology cluster, success is also limited to relatively narrow *filières,* for example the women's ready-to-wear industry where design, and the branding associated with French design in particular, are crucial elements of competitive success.[50]

Once more, *The Global Competitiveness Report* tends to confirm that national competitiveness for advanced industrial economies such as the European "Big 3" corresponds rather closely with global market share in quality-competitive high-tech industrial sectors—and, at the same time, reveals the vulnerabilities in each country's economic and social model. Its comparatively weaker competitive position in the three sectors we have reviewed is mirrored in the broader World Economic Forum assessment. France is ranked 30 in Growth Competitiveness, with only Greece and Italy among the 15 members of the EU before the 2004 enlargement ranking below France. The report affirms considerable strength in some areas of Microeconomic Competitiveness such as those associated with international distribution (2) and marketing (3), but also significant competitive disadvantages in areas such as labor-employer relations (78), corporate income tax rate (77), and government expenditure (78). It seems quite clear that there is at least an element of truth in the traditional view of the French economy as inflexible, dominated by a *dirigiste* state, and reluctant to meet globalization even half-way.

We asked above whether the "Big 3" have what it takes to sustain the European model and the answer appears in turn ambiguous, paradoxical, and somewhat ironic. The U.K., which is the least European and the most neo-liberal in its model, seems the least threatened by globalization. Will it have the political will to use its success to strengthen social protections and reduce inequalities? Despite a concerted effort by France to accommodate itself to the rigors of globalization in recent years, the evidence we have seems to indicate that the process will not be easy. Core components of the French economic and social model—the heavy role of the state and the high level and cost of social protections—run against the grain of globalization's dominant paradigm of economic liberalism. At the same time, France's comparative success in quality-competitive and high-tech industrial sectors is narrower and shallower than that of the U.K. and Germany. Germany, which exhibits in clearest form the European alternative to the American model, is also the largest economy in Europe, and the bell weather signaling the survival or demise of the European model. The German case is also the most paradoxical: it is stagnant and plagued with chronic high unemployment and, at the same time, it is immensely competitive across the board in the high-tech and quality-competitive sectors that characterize the leading edge of advanced economies.

EUROPEAN UNION— OR EUROPEAN DISCORD?

Don't expect to see the collapse of the European model anytime soon, but the pace of adjustments and antiregulatory reforms in France, Germany, and elsewhere are likely to quicken. And they are likely to be divisive at the level of national governments, spill over into EU politics, and create new layers and levels of discord in the European Union. The disagreements within Europe and between Europe and the United States over Iraq were divisive and troubling but they were externalities to the European Union's central agenda of economic integration and enlargement. As discussed above, the U.S./European divisions have already been shelved (although not resolved) and, even at the height of the division, the ties that really bind Europe and America, the ties of global economic interdependence, actually intensified.[51]

The ultimate effects of globalization on the exercise of power by European states and on the Union are not yet clear, but the European experience nevertheless provides very clear answers to our initial core questions:

1. How does globalization affect state power understood as the capacity of states to secure desirable outcomes autonomously? First, insofar as the EU is a collective regional response to the global challenges of economic interdependence in order to maximize European competitiveness—and it is this more than anything else—the EU represents an historic recognition that individual states no longer have the capacity to secure desirable outcomes autonomously. Clearly, Europeans have a different view of sovereignty than Americans have and, as frustrated as they may be with the bureaucratization and the democratic deficits that bedevil the EU, most are convinced that they have developed a better way to exercise power: through negotiation and collaboration.

2. What are the consequences of America's exercise of hegemonic power for the capacity of other states to exercise power? This is a battle Europeans fear they will lose—and have lost in the post-9/11 period and in the war in Iraq and thus far in its aftermath. Most Europeans (or at least those from Rumsfeld's "Old Europe") instinctively embrace Thesis 1 (the invisible hand thesis) that emphasizes the institutional biases in the global architecture that reinforce American hegemony. They also tend to accept the force of Thesis 2 (the contested sovereignty of the state thesis), which insists that globalization reduces the autonomous capacity of *all* states—and hope that the EU can be the instrument that forces the United States to accommodate itself to this reality! And, of course, the new 2004 members of the EU from the "New Europe" tend to hold the convictions associated with Thesis 3 (the globalization as the engine of democracy and progress thesis) and see in EU accession the proof of this thesis.

Beyond the ambit of these questions, Europe faces a set of distinct challenges and questions of its own. As we have seen, global economic competition makes it increasingly difficult for European societies to sustain elements of the European model, and states that have pooled their sovereignty in the European Union face restive domestic constituencies demanding that they deliver the goods that European citizens have been promised for more than 50 years. Against this backdrop, the European Union will face tremendous and quite possibly intractable problems.

Will enlargement over-tax the already strained institutions of the EU? Will it exacerbate the insider resentments against those newer poorer members with their hands out for development funds? At the same time, will the expansion of the European Union eastward intensify the outsider resentments against the most powerful EU countries that are likely to dominate the policy agendas and control the terms of the distributive arrangements to their own advantage for years to come?

During spring 2004 the prospects that a durable constitutional settlement would emerge out of these conflicts of interest remained clouded at best, the pessimism deepened by British Prime Minister Blair's startling decision in April 2004 that he would put the EU constitution to a vote in the U.K., where opinion runs strongly against ratification. Blair's decision spurred the demand for similar referendums in other countries, certainly delaying and perhaps imperiling ratification of any constitutional treaty, which requires unanimous approval. With Blair and Chirac openly squabbling and a deadlock looming over the weight given countries in voting rights (and hence which countries could combine to form a "blocking minority"), when the EU enlarged in May 2004 its ability to function effectively and resolve the constitutional challenges it faced were very much in doubt.

At this juncture, as George Ross observes, things changed rapidly for the better.

> [K]ey member states, France, Germany and Britain in particular, looked themselves in the mirror and recognized that a coincidence of enlargement and petty quarreling that prevented the Union from adapting its institutions to a Union of 25 members was likely to produce a catastrophic turning point for European integration.[52]

Pending ratification in each member country, the EU agreed to a constitutional treaty in June 2004. Successful governance of an enlarged EU remains to be achieved, but the EU gained credibility—and some breathing space.

It is possible that in time the multi-level governance of the European Union will effectively balance national and community interests and successfully integrate the nations and peoples of East and West into a common union. But the European Union faces very grave challenges on more fronts than ever before. The challenges of economic competitiveness and the challenges of multi-level governance have become acute and seem destined to intensify in the years ahead.

We said above that when push came to shove and the country-by-country demands of political constituencies, the competitive pressures of the global economy, and the limits on public spending enshrined in the stability and growth pact could not be reconciled; something had to give. It did: in November 2003, after it became absolutely clear that stagnating economies in France and Germany meant that they would breach the 3 percent limit on budget deficits, EU finance ministers agreed to suspend the sanctions mechanism that was in place to enforce fiscal discipline. The pact was placed on life support and a further wedge was driven between the most powerful countries (which were given a free pass for the time being) and the smaller countries (who have faced tougher treatment in the past). Nor was the situation improved by a July 2004 decision by the European

Court of Justice—the EU's highest court—that the finance ministers had acted illegally in suspending the threat of sanctions against France and Germany for violating the pact.

Germany and France had the power to bend the will of the European Union to serve their short-term needs, but not the capacity to float their social and economic models without imperiling economic and monetary union. The suspension of the stability pact exacerbated all the various tensions and resentments in the Union and solved nothing. Is this any way to run the world's greatest experiment in multi-level governance?

CHAPTER 4

East Asia:
The Paradox of State Power

From the mid-1970s through the mid-1990s the world marveled at the economic vitality and daunting success of eight high-performing Asian economies (HPAEs): Hong Kong, Indonesia, Japan, Malaysia, the Republic of Korea, Singapore, Taiwan, and Thailand. In a landmark—and controversial—study published in 1993, the World Bank sought to analyze the sources of their success. The report's title, *The East Asian Miracle* leaves little doubt about the view of global policymakers and leading academics concerning the performance, prospects, and potential demonstration effect of Asia's heralded development strategy.[1]

Eye-catching growth rates attracted international wonder and admiration. From 1973–1996, average growth rates were 6.1 percent in Hong Kong, 5.1 percent in Japan, 6.8 percent in Korea, and 5.6 percent in Thailand (compared to 0.5 percent in the U.K., 1.5 percent in France, 1.8 percent in West Germany, and 1.6 percent in the United States).[2] But fascination with East Asia's newly industrializing economies (NIEs)—the tigers of East Asia and their Southeast Asian counterparts who attempted to follow in their path*—was also spurred by a set of policy and political questions. "The East Asian NIEs appeared to pursue a more market-oriented development strategy than other developing countries," observed Stephan Haggard. "Because of their rapid and relatively egalitarian growth, they were held up by development economists and the international financial institutions as models of success. Yet there is substantial debate about how market-based the East Asian NIEs really are."[3] Hence: the paradox of state power in East Asia. Is there too much or too little government? Or both at different times—and in different countries?

---

*The term "Asian tigers" was initially applied exclusively to four newly industrializing East Asian economies: the Republic of Korea (South Korea), Taiwan, Hong Kong, and Singapore, but has often been extended to include a set of Southeast Asian countries that pursued similar development strategies in the 1980s: Indonesia, Malaysia, and Thailand. Discussions of the East Asian financial or economic crises nearly always include the Southeast Asian countries as well as Japan and China.

Government's role in East Asian development has been—and remains—contentious, pitting the "market-friendly" view (favored by many economists and the traditional stock-in-trade of the international financial institutions such as the IMF and the World Bank) against the "developmental state" view (favored by many political scientists). The market-friendly view contends that the state's role should be limited to market coordination. It should maintain macroeconomic stability and provide incentives for investment, high savings rates, and the enhancement of human capital (through education, training, and skill acquisition). But the state should not descend from the heights to intervene in particular industries, since such behavior would distort the function of the market in allocating investments and resources. At best, according to advocates of the market-friendly approach, such behavior would be irrelevant; at worst, it would become counter-productive.[4]

In contrast, according to the development state view, "market failure associated with coordinating resource mobilization, allocating investment, and promoting technological catch-up at the development stage is so pervasive that state intervention is necessary to remedy it."[5] In short: the state must regularly intervene strategically and with real effect to provide the coordination that markets often fail to provide.

Debate has raged between advocates of these two polar positions on states versus markets in East Asian development. Similarly, there is heated disagreement about the facts of the matter. How market oriented have the Asian Tigers really been? "Hong Kong never departed from a strong commitment to laissez-faire policies, but export-oriented industrialization in Korea and Taiwan involved a substantial degree of state intervention, such as continued protection and subsidies, as well as market-oriented reforms," noted one highly regarded academic specialist. "Moreover, economic reform efforts in these countries were led by strong, authoritarian governments."[6]

In the midst of these debates, the 1993 World Bank volume looked to explain not only the dramatic economic growth of the HPAEs, but also the policy implications of their relatively equitable distribution of wealth and the improvements in human welfare enjoyed by their citizens. Quite intentionally, in the 1993 report, the World Bank weighed in on the key question that concerns us here: the role and exercise of state power in the emergence of East Asia's HPAEs as highly effective actors in the global economy. In fact, the World Bank report, *The East Asian Miracle*, caused quite a stir and has been viewed as a turning point in the debate because it cut the legs out from under its own market-friendly orthodoxy. Good fundamentals in investment, savings, and an expanding base of human capital were very important in explaining success—but they were not the whole story. In most of the "miracle" economies, "the government intervened—systematically and through multiple channels—to foster development, and in some cases the development of specific industries."[7]

In a widely quoted passage the Report conceded:

[E]ach of the HPAEs maintained macroeconomic stability and accomplished three functions of growth: accumulation, efficient allocation, and rapid technological catch-up. They did this with combinations of policies, ranging from market-oriented to state-led, that varied both across economies and over time.[8]

At a stroke, the World Bank made it far harder to argue that East Asian economies prospered because their governments didn't succumb to the temptation to intervene in the affairs of the market—or that they would have grown even faster if their governments had intruded even less. "The *Miracle* makes it official that most of the high-performing Asian economies . . . have had extensive government intervention. It also grants that some of these interventions, in the areas of credit and exports, may have worked in fostering both growth and equity," observed economist Dani Rodrik. "Thanks to the *Miracle,* it will no longer be fashionable to argue that East Asian economies did so well because they had so few interventions, or that they would have grown even faster had there been less intervention."[9]

But of course, the Report, as noteworthy as it was, did not resolve the debate. In fact, the debate only intensified once the East Asian development model was battered and nearly went down when globalization's "perfect storm"—the financial crisis that erupted in July 1997—sent riptides crashing throughout the global economy.

THE ASIAN FINANCIAL AND ECONOMIC CRISIS

The Asian economic crisis did not come out of a clear blue sky. For years, the Japanese economy had been struggling against severe and unrelenting stagnation. Also, by 1996 there were signs that the "tiger" economies were becoming somewhat less fierce: there were signs of excess capacity in some sectors, earnings had peaked and were beginning to decline, exports were slowing. Perhaps most ominous, in light of what was to come, there were growing indications that the "bubble economy" in Thailand's financial and real estate sectors was stretched too thin.[10] And the peso crisis in Mexico in 1994–1995, which sent jitters across Latin America, should have served as a rather abrupt wake-up call to those who had grown complacent about the workings of the global economy. Increasing sums of public monies were spent to bail out investors and banks and the Group of 7 appeared to get the message. At the 1995 Halifax Summit, the G7 made the commitment to "avoid future Mexicos" through improved IMF supervision and enhanced resources.[11]

Nevertheless, when the Asian financial and economic crisis erupted in July 1997, it came with devastating fury and spread with almost unimaginable speed. The crisis began with an enormous run on the Thai baht which, despite a massive $26 billion intervention by the Thai government, lost nearly half its value by the end of the year. A host of neighboring countries—South Korea, Indonesia, Singapore, the Philippines—experienced much of the same pattern. "Each experienced a tidal wave of troubles centering on the rapid outflow of foreign capital, 30 to 50 percent plunges in their stock markets, and significant declines in the exchange rates of their national currencies," explained T. J. Pempel. "Most also faced banking crises, problems of short-term debt repayment, recessions, sharp decelerations in their previously soaring economic growth rates, or some combination of these. Between July 1997 and April 1998, some 150 Asian financial institutions were shut down, suspended, nationalized, or placed under the care of a government restructuring agency."[12]

It should come as no surprise that when the financial bubble burst, banks crumbled, jobs and savings were lost, massive corruption and cronyism was revealed, a lot of political bubbles exploded as well. In Indonesia, the country after Thailand that was hardest hit by the Thai currency's collapse, as urban poverty and joblessness skyrocketed, massive demonstrations and political unrest scuttled the Suharto regime.[13] The economic turmoil helped sweep leaders from office in the Philippines and South Korea and triggered internecine battles within the government and street protests in Malaysia.[14]

"The biggest lesson from Asia's troubles isn't about economics," observed Paul Krugman in his characteristically caustic style. "It's about governments. When Asian economies delivered nothing but good news, it was possible to convince yourself that the alleged planners of those economies knew what they were doing. Now the truth is revealed: They don't have a clue."[15]

Krugman's conclusion may be a little over the top, but it provides an important reminder for us: the ultimate significance of the East Asian financial and economic crisis lies in what it reveals about the role and capacity of governments and state institutions to not simply ride the waves of globalization but apply their still significant powers—if they would but use them—to achieve strategic goals. In fact, the Asian crisis of 1997–1999 has become a parable on the theme of state power and globalization. As with most parables, the truth or moral lesson is in the eye of the beholder.

The Asian Crisis: A Parable for Our Times

"The economic circumstances that led to the economic success of East Asian economies are by now reasonably well understood," observed Nobel Prize winning development economist Amartya Sen. "While different empirical studies have varied in emphasis, there is by now a fairly agreed general list of 'helpful policies' that includes openness to competition, the use of international markets, a high level of literacy and school education, successful land reforms and public provision of incentives for investment, exporting and industrialization."[16]

There is no similar consensus regarding the causes of the crisis, however, or the reason for the differential consequences for particular countries, or the effectiveness and durability of alternative development models. Most important here, the political significance of the crisis is hotly contested. What does it tell us about state power in hard times?

The East Asian crisis of 1997–1999 became a Rorschach test for interpretations of globalization and state power, a diagnostic test of alternative models. People saw in the currency and market turmoil, the string of domestic political crises, and the responses of the United States, the other G7 powers, and the institutions of global governance what their intellectual mindsets conditioned them to see.

For John Mearsheimer, neither the interdependence ascribed to globalization nor the constraints attributed to international organizations has changed the structural disposition of the international order. States remain the key actors; they operate in an anarchic system; great powers have offensive military capabilities; they must be wary of other states who may have hostile intent; they have the capacity to strategically advance their interests. From this realist perspective— one in which all states should want to achieve more power than they currently possess (the core premise of offensive realism)—Mearsheimer remains skeptical that economic interdependence makes military conflict between great powers as unlikely as many suppose. If even in the best of times, during periods when all the great powers are prospering, the structural attributes of the international system mean that war cannot be taken off the table, what are the security implications of economic crisis?[17]

As Mearsheimer explains, financial insecurity heightens the risk of geopolitical and military insecurity:

> [I]t is widely believed that Asia's "economic miracle" worked to dampen security competition in that region before 1997, but that the 1997–1998 financial crisis in Asia helped foster a "new geopolitics." It is worth noting that although the United States led a successful effort to contain that financial crisis, it was a close call, and there is no guarantee that the next crisis will not spread across the globe. But even in the absence of a major economic crisis, one or more states might not prosper; such a state would have little to lose economically, and maybe even something to gain, by starting a war.[18]

Mearsheimer finds unpersuasive any claims that the end of the Cold War introduced a fundamental change in the structural attributes of the international system. Since the global order remains anarchic and states are as willing as ever to project power for advantage, behavior is unchanged as is the potential for conflict. Even with the crisis in Asia abated, the possibilities for turmoil remain including: another cycle of deterioration or miscalculation disturbing the nuclear standoff in South Asia; a belligerent posture by China or a secessionist gesture by Taiwan; the spiraling downward of the confrontation with North Korea over nuclear weapons.[19] In the context of East Asia, Mearsheimer's realism is persuasive in associating financial crisis with geopolitical and military insecurity.

For Thomas Friedman, the Asian crisis fits the era of stampeding "Electronic Herds" and market forces trampling state power. In fact, Friedman begins *The Lexus and the Olive Tree* with his version of the East Asian financial crisis, told with his characteristic panache. In December 1997, two days after the government of Thailand went public with its decision to shut down virtually all of its key banks that were involved in international currency transactions, as Friedman tells the story, he found himself in a taxi being driven down Asoke Street, Bangkok's Wall Street. As the cab driver passed by each of the fallen financial giants, he pointed to them in turn, pronouncing each one dead.

"I did not know it at the time—no one did—but these Thai investment houses were the first dominoes in what would prove to be the first global financial crisis of the new era of globalization," observed Friedman. "The Thai crisis triggered a general flight of capital out of virtually all the Southeast Asian emerging markets, driving down the value of currencies in South Korea, Malaysia and Indonesia."[20] But the story only begins there. Friedman links the fall of the baht to the crisis in the Russian economy in 1998 and mounting problems in Brazil. He is so persuaded that the crisis reveals the core meaning of globalization for the hollowing out of state power that he uses the crisis as the opening scene of his account of globalization. For Friedman the runaway force of the Asian financial crisis proved the power of the herdlike stampedes of speculative traders, and demonstrated the incapacity of states to control markets, which are seen to behave like an irresistible force of nature.

More than any of our other interlocutors in the globalization debates, Joseph Stiglitz makes the Asian financial crisis a centerpiece of his account of globalization, and for a host of good reasons. At the time of the crisis, Stiglitz had been studying the region for a quarter-century. He had been a member of the research team for the *The East Asian Miracle* so he definitely had a horse in the race when it came to disputes about what had gone wrong. In fact, Stiglitz served as the World Bank's chief economist and senior vice president from 1997 to 2000, so it was very much on his watch that the financial crisis in East Asia exploded. In addition, Stiglitz's work in economic theory (on the dire consequences for developing countries when the implications of incomplete information, inadequate markets, and ineffective institutions are ignored) seemed tailor made to fit the circumstances of the East Asian crisis.[21]

So it comes as no surprise that alongside his critical assessment of the IMF's role in the post-Soviet marketization of Russia's economy, his critique of the Fund's handling of the East Asian crisis is the central focus of *Globalization and Its Discontents*. According to Stiglitz, both the IMF and the World Bank had run away from studying the region, only agreeing to do so under intense pressure from the Japanese backed by their willingness to pay for the study. Given that the evident success of the East Asian economies was *the* "feel good" development story of the era, what accounts for their reluctance to trumpet the regions staggering growth trajectory?

Stiglitz thought the reason was obvious, and he didn't mince words when explaining it. "The countries had been successful not only in spite of the fact that they had not followed most of the dictates of the Washington Consensus, but *because* they had not," contended Stiglitz. "Though the experts' findings were toned down in the final published report, the World Bank's Asian Miracle study laid out the important roles that the government had played. These were far from the minimalist roles beloved of the Washington Consensus."[22] Stiglitz argues that the developmental transformation in East Asia owes a great deal to state directed industrial policy and an emphasis not on opening domestic markets to foreign competition—but rather on promoting exports. Governments in East Asia worked to reduce poverty and constrain inequality in order to advance both social cohesion and a positive climate for growth-fueling investment. Both a good portion of the miracle and the recovery after the crisis can be explained by the "government-led strategies of closing the technology gap and investing heavily in human capital [that] have placed several of the countries in a position not only to avail themselves of the new technologies, but to become leaders in their exploitation."[23]

All this cut against the grain of the Washington Consensus, and the architects of that consensus, argues Stiglitz, insisted on their familiar neo-liberal palliatives once the crisis struck, which only made things far worse. As Stiglitz tells the story, the IMF (clearly the villain in the piece) and the leaders of the Asian countries were at loggerheads from the moment the crisis struck. The world financial leaders—led by an imperturbable Bill Clinton—considered the collapse of the Thai baht a minor setback, and insisted that developing countries stay the course. In the September 1997 annual meeting of the IMF and the World Bank, IMF officials urged more pressure to open capital markets to foreign participation (a central condition routinely imposed by the IMF for providing loans to developing countries).

In contrast, Asian finance ministers were terrified when they contemplated the scale of damage the financial crisis would cause their national economies and the havoc it would bring to their societies. Moreover Asian finance ministers were convinced that hot money (the quick entrance and exit of speculative financial transactions) was at the root of the crisis. In this context, observed Stiglitz:

> *They felt . . . powerless to resist. They even knew what could and should be done to prevent a crisis and minimize the damage—but they knew the IMF would condemn them if they undertook those actions and they feared the resulting withdrawal of international capital. In the end, only Malaysia was*

brave enough to risk the wrath of the IMF; and though Prime Minister Mahathir's policies—trying to keep interest rates low, trying to put brakes on the rapid flow of speculative money out of the country—were attacked from all quarters, Malaysia's downturn was shorter and shallower than that of any of the other countries.[24]

For Stiglitz, the IMF's worst blunder was its inability to see the need for proper "sequencing and pacing."[25] Stiglitz argues that the dictum that markets work as if by an invisible hand—the financial world according to Adam Smith and Thomas Friedman—applies under very restrictive conditions. "[M]ore recent advances in economic theory," argues Stiglitz, no doubt including his own research, "have shown that whenever information is imperfect and markets incomplete, which is to say always, *and especially in developing countries,* then the invisible hand works most imperfectly."[26] The IMF and the United States neglected the social and political context and forced market liberalization in the East Asian developing countries before the necessary regulatory framework was in place and before these countries could weather the speculative shocks. Stiglitz concludes with evident passion, "I believe that capital account liberalization was *the single most important factor leading to the crisis.*"[27]

Implications for Understanding East Asian States

The very different perspectives on the East Asian financial crisis provided by Mearsheimer, Friedman, and Stiglitz (and a great many other academics and policymakers) make it clear that the debate still rages, with no end in sight. The nineteenth-century philosopher G. W. F. Hegel noted in the *Philosophy of Right,* his treatise on the state, "the owl of Minerva spreads its wings only with the falling of the dusk."[28] Hegel meant that philosophy comes to understand a way of life just as it passes from view, but the same may be said about state power in the twilight of crisis and, still later, in the early years of recovery. When the East Asian crisis hit, why was the crisis so uneven in its consequences—some countries persevering reasonably well and others suffering economic calamity compounded by significant political turmoil?[29] What are the implications of the East Asian miracle, the crisis, and the recovery for understanding the interactive effects of globalization and state power?

To shed light on these questions, Korea is the place to start, since its extraordinary success in economic growth and competitiveness in the past 50 years has made it the cause célèbre for every controversy about alternative East Asian development models and a watershed case for the shifting fortunes of laissez-faire and state-interventionist models. We look to state power—its general institutional weakness or its "hollowing out" under the acute pressures of liberalization and crisis—as a key part of the explanation of why some states (such as Korea) proved to be more vulnerable than others (such as Taiwan).

The stakes are high and the debate—one in which specialists have staked out refined positions that hinge on discriminating conceptual distinctions and fine-grained close historical analyses of national cases—extremely complex. For our purposes, we can start from an important uncontested premise: that South Korea has been what has traditionally been called a "strong state": a state that can effectively interact with social forces and act with effect, discretion, and a degree of autonomy as an agent at once of class power and of the nation's citizens, and to balance the two.[30] Certainly, at the least, the Korean state "has been anything but minimalist; not only has it been involved extensively in every sphere of economic activity, but a compelling case has been made that this involvement was in large measure responsible for the remarkable economic success of the country."[31]

But as the crisis approached, the effectiveness and capacity of the Korean state had receded. Meredith Woo-Cumings explains that the difficulties of the developmental state in Korea stem from the convoluted dynamics in the relationship between the state and entrepreneurs. "In Korea, politics were hostage to economics—and more," observes Woo-Cumings. "A developmental state like Korea's creates a permanent bind for itself with regard to big business. . . . [T]he state has had to intervene to rescue the *chaebol*[†] in distress, in order to prevent the collapse of the banking system as well as massive unemployment."[32]

Through the 1980s, the Korean state was a "relentless nag, trying to force firms to reform,"[33] and attempting to control the *chaebol* through regulation. Hence the state served as both regulator and guarantor of the corporate sector as the elites were subject to cronyism—and beyond that, they were more inclined to use the state to force reorganization than to trust the market to inspire reform-minded behavior.

In the 1990s, a number of factors colluded to erode the capacity of the state (and the willingness of political elites) to effectively regulate the corporate and financial sectors and, in particular, its control of finance and credit. The pressure from international organizations for an accelerated pace in financial deregulation was a factor, and this external pressure was reinforced by pressure at home from the powerful *chaebol* to eliminate barriers to their full participation in the financial sector. The financial supervisory authority was split between the Ministry of Finance and the Bank of Korea. In addition, the Economic Planning Board was dismantled. The state's capacity to coordinate industrial plans or strategically channel investment and regulate financial flows were reduced to a bare minimum.

Thus when the crisis hit, Korea was extremely vulnerable. As Linda Weiss put it bluntly, "In the Korean case, it was not institutionalized weakness *per se*

[†]The *chaebol* is an extensive conglomerate of many companies clustered around one parent company, which does business under integrated financial and managerial control in multiple markets, and often exhibits a considerable degree of family control.

but the gradual decomposition of core capacities that paved the way for the high-risk borrowing strategies and over-investment of the *chaebol,* which then exposed Korea to sudden downturns and capital flight."[34]

Not so in Taiwan. Certainly, as Stephen Haggard observes, Taiwan was left relatively unscathed by the financial crisis because of strong fundamental economics. "Taiwan makes abundantly clear that vulnerability to crisis depends in the first instance on a country's debt and reserve position," and Taiwan was sheltered from the financial storm by "the absence of significant external debt and abundant reserves."[35] But as Haggard acknowledges and other observers emphasize, political factors associated with the state's capacity to intervene and shape institutional and market outcomes were also extremely important.

Perhaps most importantly, Taiwan got Stiglitz's sequencing right. The government and the Central Bank of China (CBC) developed a resilient regulatory regime that controlled the flow of capital from financial sectors into real estate; cooled down the bubble economy; and "brought an overheated stock market and real estate sector partially under control before the regional financial crisis broke out."[36]

In Taiwan's case, its peculiar geopolitical circumstances—the exclusion from the IMF and the World Bank (since 1978), the ever-present potential of economic sanctions instigated by China, the incessant diplomatic tension—have created a mindset and a determination in Taiwan to create an extensive "shock-absorbing capacity."[37] Hence the goals and institutional capacities of the Taiwanese state remained intact into the 1990s. "In spite of the growing importance of liberal economic ideas in Taiwan's public discourse, it is likely that the continuing geopolitical threat (the China question), together with Taiwan's peculiar diplomatic isolation, served as important countervailing pressures that tempered and moderated the domestic push to embrace economic liberalism," observes Weiss. "As a result, state actors in Taiwan by and large continued to view the state both as an important goal setter for the national economy and as an indispensable means of sustaining an internationally competitive industry."[38]

In their paths to development—and under the exacting conditions imposed by the Asian financial crisis—Korea took a more state-minimizing direction and Taiwan a more state-enhancing path. Five years after the crisis abated, both countries displayed considerable strength in their abilities to effectively navigate the often-treacherous waters of the global economy. But Taiwan's economy was more competitive than Korea's due in no small measure to the enduring legacy of its effective interventionist regime.

In the aftermath of the crisis, the Korean state, having lost its innocence about economic policy, took pragmatic steps to regain the initiative. "It is bereft of the innocent exuberance often found in the proponents of industrial policy, extolling the virtues of developmental coordination between the state and the enterprises," observed Meredith Woo-Cumings. "But it is also bereft of innocence with regard to laissez-faire. Instead, the thrust of the reform has been profoundly practical, mixing the exigency of liberal reform with heavy-handed industrial reorganization to force private sector restructuring."[39] As the Economic Integration section of the *Republic of Korea Global Profile* indicates, exports and imports each comprise over 40 percent of the country's GDP, remarkably high figures that suggest Korea is fully—and rather effectively—engaged in the global economy.

The *Global Competitiveness Report, 2002–2003* ranked Korea 21 in Growth Competitiveness with very high scores in the quality of the national business environment and in several technology components of growth competitiveness.[40] In 2003, expanded trade between Japan, China, and South Korea—accounting for roughly one-fifth of the three countries' export totals for the year confirmed the fact that Northeast Asia was "an increasingly powerful and integrated part of the world economy."[41]

On the role of the state, the pragmatic approach identified by Woo-Cumings appeared to prevail, but the rhetoric was heating up. After foreign-owned banks failed to heed the government's call for a bailout of Korea's largest credit card company, the new finance minister, observing that "the market is not a children's playground where you only do things that you like," lambasted "selfish" financial institutions for threatening market stability.[42] In short, there were indications that it might not prove easy for Korea to balance an interventionist approach to economic management with the neo-liberal dictates of the global market.

Meanwhile, The *Global Competitiveness Report, 2002–2003* ranked Taiwan third in the world in its Growth Competitiveness rankings, with very high scores in technology related criteria, the quality of the microeconomic business environment, and subsidies and tax credits for firm level R & D, among quite a few other top ten rankings.[43] Taiwan's stock market was Asia's best performer in the first quarter of 2004, its growth forecast was surpassing 5 percent and, with exports representing roughly half of the GDP, Taiwan's central bank was intervening aggressively to control the rise of the Taiwan dollar.[44]

The Implications for Globalization and State Power

What are the implications of these two cases—South Korea and Taiwan—for our broader understanding of globalization and state power? Although only very rough cross-regional comparisons are possible, it is worth noting that both in Europe and in Asia we find examples of more state-interventionist models (Taiwan, France, and Germany) and more market-friendly models (the United Kingdom and the Republic of Korea).

Against the expectations of the Washington Consensus and neo-liberal orthodoxy, Taiwan stands out as a telling counter-example of a country that has applied a state-interventionist and aggressive regulatory regime to an extremely successful position in global competitiveness. With his hands full, facing restive constituencies at home and having to contend with increasingly complex and

FIGURE 4.1
Republic of Korea Global Profile

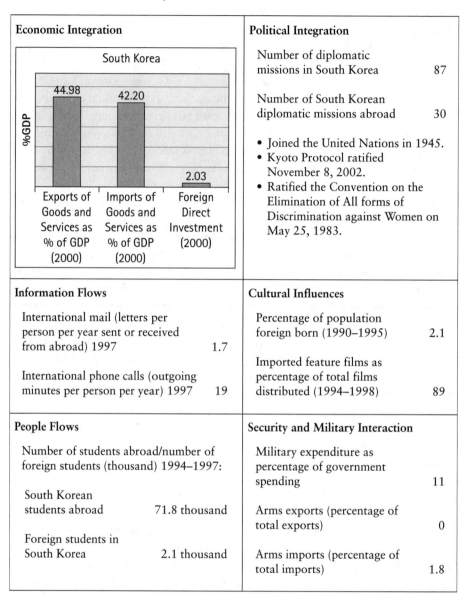

Economic Integration

South Korea

44.98   42.20

2.03

| Exports of Goods and Services as % of GDP (2000) | Imports of Goods and Services as % of GDP (2000) | Foreign Direct Investment (2000) |

%GDP

Political Integration

Number of diplomatic
missions in South Korea   87

Number of South Korean
diplomatic missions abroad   30

• Joined the United Nations in 1945.
• Kyoto Protocol ratified
  November 8, 2002.
• Ratified the Convention on the
  Elimination of All forms of
  Discrimination against Women on
  May 25, 1983.

Information Flows

International mail (letters per
person per year sent or received
from abroad) 1997   1.7

International phone calls (outgoing
minutes per person per year) 1997   19

Cultural Influences

Percentage of population
foreign born (1990–1995)   2.1

Imported feature films as
percentage of total films
distributed (1994–1998)   89

People Flows

Number of students abroad/number of
foreign students (thousand) 1994–1997:

South Korean
students abroad   71.8 thousand

Foreign students in
South Korea   2.1 thousand

Security and Military Interaction

Military expenditure as
percentage of government
spending   11

Arms exports (percentage of
total exports)   0

Arms imports (percentage of
total imports)   1.8

unforgiving internecine battles in the European Union, it is unlikely that Germany's Gerhard Schröder is paying much attention to Taiwan's impressive World Economic Forum rankings or growth rates. But the case of Taiwan and the evident strengths of Germany's "high-everything" economy (which remains extremely competitive across the board in high-tech quality-goods sectors) should provide some pause for those who consider the state increasingly impotent in the face of imperious economic forces. As Taiwan and Germany demonstrate, state capacities for sustained strategic interventions in the economy matter. Countries with effective regulatory regimes anchored in their political cultures, social and economic models, and geopolitical circumstances may beat the odds in global competition.

Recall our first core question: How does globalization (in this case, the challenges of economic competitiveness) affect state power understood as the capacity of states to secure desirable outcomes? Comparative analysis of the Asian economic crisis reveals a very important answer: the capacity of states to secure desirable outcomes depends on the ability of states to marshal effective and sustained strategic interventions in order to respond effectively to external shocks, maintain technological competitiveness, sustain investment, and effectively coordinate economic responses to a changing environment.[45] States matter, but different states can affect outcomes to different degrees and with differential effect in particular policy arenas. This Asian case study makes another important contribution to the book's argument. It presents a strong vote for Thesis 2 (the contested sovereignty of the state thesis) by affirming the claim that globalization does not uniformly weaken states, but rather creates a set of challenges to which states must respond—and they do so in particular ways with varying success.

Looking beyond the domestic configurations of state power and capacity, it is worth recalling Mearsheimer's observation that the East Asian financial crisis also had geopolitical reverberations, a point that is certainly not lost on the Taiwanese. When it comes to the People's Republic of China, to which we now turn, there is no mistaking the interplay of geopolitical power and economic interdependence today, especially with regard to the increasingly pivotal matter of U.S./China relations.

CHINA: WHEN GEOPOLITICS TRUMPS TRADE

If anyone doubted the depth, strategic importance, and shifting tides of U.S./China relations, the visit to Washington by the Chinese Prime Minister Wen Jiabao in December 2003, should have dispelled those doubts. Despite continued complaints from textile and apparel industry association representatives that Chinese imports were the primary cause of job losses and a drumbeat of angry congressional voices demanding redress for their constituents, both sides played down the trade dispute and concentrated on bigger strategic themes.

In geopolitical terms, with the pot still boiling over in Iraq, the Bush administration needed the diplomatic support of China as a permanent member of the United Nations Security Council (or at least its willingness to steer clear of the foot-dragging of "Old Europe") on any new initiative to restore order or smooth the transition to international or Iraqi authority. Likewise, the United States has a big stake in Beijing's willingness to play a productive role in controlling North Korea's nuclear weapons program through bilateral diplomatic efforts with Pyongyang and in its role to coordinate six-way regional talks to break the U.S./North Korean stalemate. In return for tacit or explicit support on these key post-9/11 American priorities—and the significant broad-based support offered by China for international antiterror efforts—the Bush administration was more than willing to play down its routine penny-ante trade squabbles and to mute its objections to Chinese human rights abuses.

In fact Wen was a big winner: gaining the prestige and visibility of a rare 19-gun salute on the south lawn of the White House (Bush's first such honor for a head of government as distinct from a head of state) and far more importantly gaining an historic shift in America's two-China policy. In the week before Wen's visit to Washington, Taiwan's president Chen Shui-bian announced that he would conduct a referendum in March 2004 (at the same time as the presidential election) that offered the voters the opportunity to demand that China remove the 500 ballistic missiles aimed at Taiwan. Why shouldn't Chen, like any politician, play to his base? The announcement of a referendum may have been a good bet to mobilize his supporters in the Democratic Progressive party, many of whom back independence from China. But as a high stakes geopolitical gamble it nearly wiped out the Taiwanese president.

The Bush administration considered Chen's announcement to be a provocation (they may well have been irritated at the timing) and reacted in dramatic fashion. With Wen at his side, President Bush rebuked Chen Shui-bian for his referendum gambit. More significantly, the United States renounced its historic policy of "strategic ambiguity"—America's refusal to specify what its reaction might be to a move by Taiwan to affirm independence or by China to absorb Taiwan. The administration removed a good portion of the ambiguity by asserting that the United States would oppose any unilateral attempt to change the status quo. Bush made clear that he opposed even the limited and democratic step in a process that might or might not lead to change in the status quo represented by the referendum; and, at the same time, declared that Beijing and Washington were now "partners in diplomacy."

In the end, Chen won re-election in the bizarre and disputed March 2004 election by an extremely small margin, after being grazed by a bullet shortly before the election, and amidst massive protests. Despite support by more than 80 percent of those casting ballots for two referendum questions demanding concessions from China, neither measure achieved the required percentage of eligible

Despite trade disputes and powerful support in Congress for pro-independence move-
ments in Taiwan, President Bush rolled out the red carpet for the December 2003 visit by
China's prime minister, Wen Jiabao.
Kevin 'KAL' Kallaugher, *The Economist,* December 13, 2003, p. 29.

voters for passage. After the election, Chen moved quickly to reassure China by
immediately communicating a message of peace and pragmatism. Then, in
August 2004, Taiwan's parliament effectively scuttled the threat of any future
plebiscite on a new constitution—which might be interpreted by China as a declaration of independence—by requiring the support of a three-quarters legislative
majority, a result viewed as almost unthinkable. Once the United States, Taiwan's
most critical ally and sole protector staked out its position, Chen's climb done
was all but inevitable.

Predictably, Bush's recalibration of the two-China policy in the direction that
suited China and cut the legs out from under the Taiwanese president infuriated some
of Bush's neo-conservative minions who railed against the president's willingness
to appease dictators. Others were still fuming about the apparent willingness of

the White House to see the evisceration of the textile and apparel industry in the South and to acquiesce to a trade policy that favored the interests of giant multi-nationals (such as Boeing, Citibank, Dell, General Electric, and General Motors) over the smaller struggling textile firms and the working families they sustained against increasingly long odds.

These and dozens of other U.S.-based multinational companies have a stake in China as America's fastest growing export market, in the role of Chinese companies as key parts suppliers and participants in global production chains, and in expanded access to financial and credit card markets. As the Economic Integration section of the *China Global Profile* indicates, China is thoroughly integrated into the world economy. With exports accounting for fully one-quarter of China's massive GDP and imports amounting to one-fifth of the country's GDP, U.S.-based multinationals have become increasingly reliant on China's market for American goods as well as on the imports of Chinese manufactured products as a significant part of their "global factory" supply chain. It is no wonder that these major corporate players have become potent allies for China inside the beltway.

The hemorrhaging of textile jobs in the South—which many doubt any change in China trade policy will staunch—is of no concern to these global players, although the White House couldn't help but be concerned about the soft-on-China bashing that was certain to fuel congressional election campaigns for years to come and to mobilize the Democratic base well beyond the 2004 presidential election. Many (including former Bush administration Treasury Secretary Paul O'Neill[46]) have argued that more than many previous administrations, the Bush White House subordinates policy to politics, but there is a lot more at play in China policy than narrow political calculation.

Despite their common heritage as communist-party states, China is not Cuba. It has been said that presidents don't have a Cuba policy, they have a Florida policy—and since the 2000 presidential election, with the country held to ransom by local election officials, and a few hundred votes determining the outcome, this is probably truer than ever. But the United States can't help but have a proper China policy because of China's strategic geopolitical importance that is powerfully enhanced by its growing economic muscle. The case of U.S./China relations makes it very clear that globalization exposes even an unrivaled hegemonic state to potential vulnerabilities.

Financial Times columnist Martin Wolf rather ominously observed:

> *Today, fortunately, a symbiotic relationship exists between China and the US. The latter sends, while the former lends. The US pursues aggressive monetary easing, while China curbs US inflation. Both sides obtain what they want: Americans spend more than they earn; China enjoys the security of its reserves. But this marriage of convenience contains the seed of a bitter divorce: the growing bilateral US trade deficit with China is open to populist*

FIGURE 4.2
China Global Profile

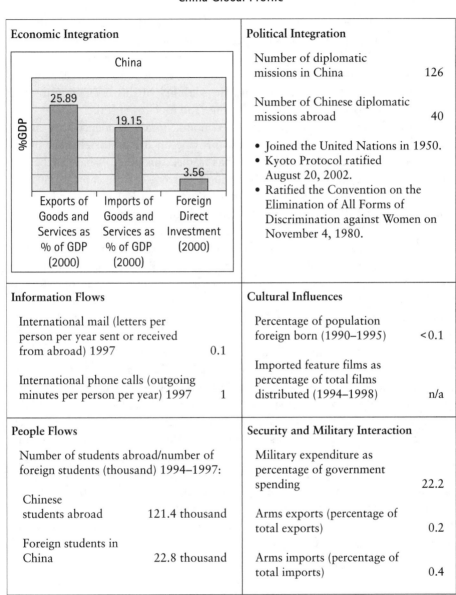

Economic Integration

China

%GDP

25.89 — Exports of Goods and Services as % of GDP (2000)

19.15 — Imports of Goods and Services as % of GDP (2000)

3.56 — Foreign Direct Investment (2000)

Political Integration

Number of diplomatic missions in China 126

Number of Chinese diplomatic missions abroad 40

- Joined the United Nations in 1950.
- Kyoto Protocol ratified August 20, 2002.
- Ratified the Convention on the Elimination of All Forms of Discrimination against Women on November 4, 1980.

Information Flows

International mail (letters per person per year sent or received from abroad) 1997 .... 0.1

International phone calls (outgoing minutes per person per year) 1997 1

Cultural Influences

Percentage of population foreign born (1990–1995) .... <0.1

Imported feature films as percentage of total films distributed (1994–1998) .... n/a

People Flows

Number of students abroad/number of foreign students (thousand) 1994–1997:

Chinese students abroad .... 121.4 thousand

Foreign students in China .... 22.8 thousand

Security and Military Interaction

Military expenditure as percentage of government spending 22.2

Arms exports (percentage of total exports) 0.2

Arms imports (percentage of total imports) 0.4

exploitation, while the US current account deficit makes the world's key currency vulnerable to an inflationary collapse.[47]

There is something about an annual U.S. trade deficit to China of $125–$130 billion that captures the attention of policy makers even during election seasons. The importance of China to American geopolitical interests and economic stability—as well as the importance of U.S./China relations to global governance, international security, and the viability of the WTO—means that China policy transcends retail electioneering. Too much is at stake.

The vulnerabilities that flow from economic interdependence that are so vividly disclosed by U.S./China relations provide an important element in our answer to the second core question that has framed this book. What are the consequences of America's exercise of hegemonic power—for the capacity of other states to exercise power, for the shape of the geopolitical order, and for the United States itself? Economic interdependence requires that the concept of hegemony must be qualified. The United States is unrivaled in military capabilities. It retains the strategic capacity to largely set global agendas and bend the key institutions of economic and political governance to its will. But, despite the superior competitiveness and overall dominance of the U.S. economy, as the story of U.S./China relations (as well as the trade wars with the EU that seem to find the United States increasingly on the losing side) reveal, the United States is vulnerable in significant ways.

Does America have the state capacity to marshal sustained strategic interventions in order to respond effectively to external shocks and coordinate economic responses to a changing environment? No: that is not the American way. But it is an extraordinary successful example of the neoliberal model and, quite clearly, its hegemonic power in military and geopolitical terms brings considerable economic benefits. Are those benefits enough to maintain the expected level of competitiveness, growth, and stability despite trade and budget deficits and relatively weak steering capacity? Thesis 1 (the invisible hand thesis) would suggest that the advantages bestowed on the United States by the global economic architecture might well be enough to offset any domestic institutional deficiencies at home. Global economic governance provides the capacity needed to sustain America's competitive edge.

THE GOOD OLD DAYS?

Europe faces unprecedented pressures to hold its Union together and make multi-level governance work. Having run the gamut from miracle to crisis to recovery, East Asian countries must struggle to refine the development models that have served them well—but also left them exposed to finance and economic crisis. The story of U.S./China relations underscores the deepening dependencies that now beset even the unrivaled hegemonic state as jobs migrate to lower wage economies, trade and budget deficits mount, and constituencies grumble. And yet, these "normal" problems of competitiveness and state capacity in the face of globalization seem like the good old days in retrospect.

As if these problems of governance and economic competitiveness were not enough, global politics took a decided turn for the worse with the terror attacks of September 11, 2001. The terrible events of 9/11 have not changed everything, but they have recast the challenges of globalization and placed renewed emphasis on terror, security, and the use of force.

PART II

GLOBAL POLITICS
POST-9/11

CHAPTER 5

Terror, War, and the Prospects of Collective Security

Through much of the mid-1990s, the most profound and deeply troubling question about globalization concerned the yawning chasm between rich and poor—the fear that the diffusion of trade, investment, production, and communication technologies had done nothing to close the gap between the developed world of Europe, America, and a powerful East Asian trading bloc on the one side, and the rest of the developing world on the other. The financial and economic crisis in East Asia in 1997 and 1998 and its rapid global diffusion seemed to intensify concerns about the dislocating effects of economic globalization, as did the tumultuous protests at the 1999 WTO ministerial meetings in Seattle.

At the same time, brutal brushfire wars and ethnic conflagrations—the bloody street fighting between Somali warlords and UN peacekeeping forces in Somalia in 1993 leading to the brutal killing of 18 American soldiers, the Rwandan genocide launched in 1994—began to capture the world's attention. Looked at from this perspective, the attacks of September 11, 2001, and the fears, threats, and experiences of terrorism ever since—whether in Jerusalem, Jakarta, Riyadh, or Madrid—seem of a piece with the political violence unleashed by the storms of ethnic, religious, and nationalist violence that accompanied the intensified combat over the state during the implosion of post-communist and post-colonial regimes in the 1990s. Against this backdrop of violence and terror, attention has naturally turned to concerns about security, war, and the implications of a new hard power American empire.

Of course, the rise of ethnic-cultural strife doesn't mean that the potentially destabilizing pressures of the globalized economy have abated. Even wealthy economies in democratic countries can't deliver full employment, keep citizens safe from crime and physical assaults, guarantee the value of investments and provide first rate education and health care. They can't float pension schemes that can keep an expanding elderly population, which is surviving longer and longer—and supported by a smaller and smaller cohort of workers—living in the manner to which they have become accustomed. Meanwhile, many states of the developing world can't protect citizens from civil strife, can't provide even rudimentary defense against plagues or famine, can't or won't extend literacy to the majority of citizens or even minimally empower women, can't reduce infant mortality rates or, in some cases, provide sufficient potable water.

Some have protested that the United States has distorted the global agenda through self-absorption and weak leadership. "By far the hardest challenge facing the world today is to keep long-term goals in mind in the face of urgent and bitter divisions over Iraq and the war on terrorism," wrote economist Jeffrey Sachs who helped implement "shock therapy" marketization to post-communist Eastern Europe in the 1990s and now argues for sustainable development. "The problems of AIDS, poverty and environmental degradation will not wait for a new consensus on Iraq or the Middle East."[1] In a similar vein, the World Bank president insisted in April 2004 that the problems of poverty and development warranted urgent and sustained attention. "There is no doubt that today the priority is being given, and maybe correctly so, to terror, to conflict," observed John D. Wolfensohn. "I would argue that there is also a need for a parallel and equally urgent attention to the question of development as a way to prevent terror, and to prevent conflict—and I really passionately believe that."[2] Multilateral development agencies, including the World Bank, remain committed to the UN Millennium Development Goals to eradicate hunger and poverty, reduce child mortality, promote the empowerment of women, and ensure environmental sustainability. But it is a sign of the times—and the preoccupations of great power politics especially since the attacks of September 11, 2001—that concern for development is often sold as an antiterrorism strategy.

The enduring question of how America and the world can—and should—meet the security threats of the post-9/11 world have risen to the very top of the agenda of global politics. Hence this theme will frame Part 3. In this chapter we will consider two central questions posed by the contemporary moment of globalization: How should the United States and the international community define and prosecute the war on terrorism? What are the lessons of the war in Iraq for the role of the Security Council in authorizing the use of force—and what reforms should now be given serious consideration? In Chapter 6, we will turn to the implications of the new American empire for understanding globalization and its consequences for state power.

Whether in Iraq, the Middle East more generally, the Korean peninsula, West Africa, Haiti, or anywhere else Washington decides to direct its gaze, the American projection of power—instinctively unilateralist and unfailingly exercised on its own terms even when ad-hoc multilateralism prevails—dominates the foreign policy horizon. Hence, America's role in meeting the security threat since September 11, 2001, and, more specifically, in launching the invasion of Iraq and controlling the torturous postwar exercise loom large in the discussion that follows.[3] Like the famous statue of Saddam Hussein, with the lasso tossed around its neck by jubilant American troops, tottering for a moment, before crashing to the ground, we are poised in a moment of uncertainty, knowing that inescapable change lies just ahead, but not knowing the precise contours of change. But unlike the historic image in April 2003 that was flashed instantly around the world to herald the end of the Baathist regime, the remorseless and violent drudgery of occupation and resistance inspires no jubilation—and it provides no assurances about what the future will bring either for the people of Iraq or for their counterparts across the globe whose sense of security and safety has been irretrievably lost. Will the diplomatic debacles at the United Nations in the run-up to war, the crescendo of violence and mayhem after the transfer of authority to an interim government in June 2004, and the urgent need for UN leadership and broad international support if there is to be any hope for stabilizing Iraq create the impetus for Security Council reform? What lessons will be learned about the prospects and consequences of a new American empire from the excruciating difficulties of bringing stability and democracy through invasion and regime change in Iraq?

Whatever else may result from the war in Iraq, the way the Iraqi story is written will powerfully shape our assessment of alternative strategies that may be deployed to meet the security threat of the post-9/11 era of global politics. This period of intensified attention to security, war, and the stultifying problems of Iraqi reconstruction also invite a fundamental reappraisal of globalization and an assessment of how hard power issues recast state politics in this daunting era.

We begin by revisiting the first principles and decisive early decisions made in the immediate aftermath of the terror attacks on the World Trade Center.

THE WAR ON TERRORISM: A DANGEROUS METAPHOR?

The attacks of September 11, 2001, ended America's instinctive belief that it was impervious to attacks from abroad. These horrendous attacks, coming literally out of a clear blue sky, stirred haunting fears of faceless enemies and unimagined vulnerabilities beyond the protection of the world's mightiest military garrison. Americans took the attacks personally, as an affront to the nation and a challenge to their way of life. How could they not?

But the world community would formally lay claim to the universal horrors of September 11. The very next day, by invoking Article 5 of the Washington Treaty, NATO rendered the attack on the United States an attack on all alliance members, and the UN Security Council cast the attacks in New York, Washington, and Pennsylvania as "a threat to international peace and security." And a good case could be made that these attacks were different than previous terrorist attacks—such as those in London, Belfast, Moscow, and Madrid (in 2000)—in scale and ambition, scope and consequences.[4] Members of an international network perpetrated these terror attacks, nationals of dozens of countries were murdered, and the repercussions for international stability were immense.

But for Americans, it was about America, a point instinctively captured by Jean-Marie Colombani in the September 12 issue of *Le Monde:* "In this tragic moment, when words seem so inadequate to express the shock people feel, the first thing that comes to mind is this: We are all Americans! We are all New Yorkers." America would not hesitate to defend itself. There was no doubt that the United States would react quickly and with vengeful force, but how and to what effect?

After some initial fleeting references to criminality, the official rhetoric of war very quickly took hold. By 8:30 P.M. on the evening of September 11, in his address to the nation, President Bush decisively established the frame of reference: "We will make no distinction between the terrorist who committed these acts and those who harbor them." And, in the climax of his address, just before his emotional appeal for prayers on behalf of the grieving families, the President declared, "America and our friends and allies join with all those who want peace and security in the world, and we stand together to win the war against terrorism."[5]

It soon became clear that for President Bush war was no metaphor. The war on terrorism would not be a rhetorical rallying cry for sustained and focused attention to a great national problem as in normal times. The war on terrorism would not be like a war on crime or a war on drugs. Within ten days of the attacks, just war theorist Michael Walzer noted regretfully, "Military action is what everybody wants to talk about—not the metaphor of war, but the real thing."[6] Walzer argued that three efforts in keeping with a metaphorical call to arms should precede any serious cry for a real war: "intensive police work across national borders, an ideological campaign to engage all the arguments and excuses for terrorism and reject them, and a serious and sustained diplomatic effort."

But the decision against this more deliberate more metaphorical approach had already been made. The attacks were acts of war. Their perpetrators were not soldiers or participants in an international criminal conspiracy. They were terrorists. To win this war against terrorism required more than homeland security, it required a total victory defined as the physical annihilation of both the terrorists and their structures of support, including the regimes of states that harbored them.

More systematically than Walzer, British military historian Michael Howard has made the case against this approach, characterizing it as "a very natural but terrible and irrevocable error." Howard argued that British experience reveals that many such "wars" can be effectively prosecuted—in Ireland, Palestine, Cyprus, and Malaya (the modern Malaysia)—when cast as "emergencies" requiring concerted action and the use of force short of war. For Howard, the repeated public assertion that America was at war was counter-productive, imperiling the entire campaign, inspiring a "war psychosis" that demanded immediate, spectacular results, and accounts of heroism.

Real war requires an identifiable, hostile adversary that looks a lot like a traditional state, while an effective campaign against a transnational terror network requires a very different, more below the media radar, approach that relies on "secrecy, intelligence, political sagacity, quiet ruthlessness, covert actions that remain covert, above all infinite patience." Howard strongly suggested that the defiant promise of a war on terror makes the subtler more strategic approach all but impossible, and exposed any who question the immediate use of overwhelming military force to accusations of appeasement. Howard concluded, "many people would have preferred a police operation conducted under the auspices of the United Nations on behalf of the international community as a whole, against a criminal conspiracy whose members should be hunted down and brought before an international court, where they would receive a fair trial and, if found guilty, be awarded an appropriate sentence."[7]

It is understandable that neither the country's leadership nor ordinary Americans had the patience or the desire to meet an attack experienced as a second Pearl Harbor by proxy or through quiet, lengthy, and inconclusive criminal investigations and juridical procedures. Bin Laden would not be turned into Milošević, Americans cheated of the opportunity to use their massive military superiority to avenge the catastrophic terror attack on the nation. If ever there was a time for the direct and uncompromising use of force this was it.

George Bush himself made the key opening statements that defined the war on terrorism in a brief radio address to the American people on September 15 and to Congress on September 20. "Victory against terrorism," the President told a radio audience on September 15 that was still reeling from the shock of the attacks , "will not take place in a single battle, but in a series of decisive actions against terrorist organizations and those who harbor and support them."[8] He confirmed a few days later that the use of force would be long, difficult, and sustained. "Our war on terror begins with al-Qaeda," the President informed a defiant Congress on September 20 and a worldwide audience that harbored little doubt about America's military resolve, "but it does not end there. It will not end until every terrorist group of global reach has been found, stopped and defeated."[9]

The President cautioned, as did other senior officials repeatedly, that this war would be like no other: "It will not look like the air war above Kosovo two years ago, where no ground troops were used and not a single American was lost in combat. Our response involves far more than instant retaliation and isolated strikes. Americans should not expect one battle, but a lengthy campaign, unlike any other we have ever seen."[10] But Americans were not invited to contemplate the possibility that casting the counter-terror mobilization as war and, moreover, as a war under the sole authority and direction of the United States, might jeopardize the campaign.

In short order, the United States declined NATO's offer to act on its commitment to collective self-defense, and never took what would have been an easy and wholly uncontroversial diplomatic gesture to recognize the formal authority of the Security Council regarding the use of force and request its authorization to respond the attacks of September 11.[11] It is understandable that in taking the attacks personally, America wanted to respond in kind—decisively, in a manner of its own choosing, answerable to none. America's response was understandable—but counterproductive, for reasons Americans also understood instinctively but were inclined to suppress in their fury and horror.

The attacks of September 11 were unique among acts of terrorism. The World Trade Center was just that—a unique locus for global commerce and finance—based in New York, but not of New York like Coney Island or Yankee Stadium. The destruction of the World Trade Center was more like an attack on the United Nations or the World Bank—a physical assault on citizens and elite representatives of countries that spread loss and fear across the globe and a symbolic attack on the institutionalized networks of international business and finance: the public face of globalization.

As one observer noted:

> [T]he attacks on New York and Washington . . . are different from those that have plagued London, Belfast, Madrid, and Moscow. Those unlawful acts were designed to change a particular policy, but not destroy a social organization. The ambition, scope, and intended fallout of the acts of September 11 make them an aggression, initially targeting the United States but aimed, through these and subsequent acts, at destroying the social and economic structures and values of a system of world public order, along with the international law that sustains it.[12]

Singular in scope, design, and significance, the terror attacks of 9/11 invited a unique—and uniquely collective—response. The effective prosecution of the campaign against international terrorists begged for a robust exercise in collective self-defense. Strategic cross-border terror constitutes a fundamental assault on every member of the international community. It represents a profound challenge to the system of collective security established by the UN Charter and should be faced head on as such. Nothing less than a collaborative and multifaceted strategic mobilization at the level of regional and international organizations holds much chance of success. And the response must include ideological, diplomatic, geopolitical, investigative, judicial, and military dimensions.

It is impossible to inoculate the world from every terrorist act, but the frequency and strategic effect of terrorism can be blunted: it is possible to disrupt and disable terror networks and intensify both incentives and pressures in an effort to deter states from harboring terror networks. The remedy is not less force than a "war on terrorism" but more effective, better targeted, clearly defined use of force within a broader geopolitical, diplomatic, and investigative strategy. In short, despite the difficulties associated with Security Council authorization (which will be discussed in detail below) no effort should be spared to garner international legitimacy for any use of force in response to 9/11. For that is the precondition for building the kind of coalition—not so much a coalition of the willing as an effective regional and cross-cultural coalition—that would exponentially increase the prospects for success.

In this era of ferocious intrastate wars born of ethnic and nationalist conflicts and growing pressure for military intervention for humanitarian purposes, the motives for great power interventions are both complex and suspect. Likewise, the effectiveness and legitimacy of humanitarian intervention, as we shall see, are subject to very different interpretations. But this much is clear: whether they are invasions or humanitarian interventions or the necessary product of a war against terrorism, great power incursions in Kosovo, Afghanistan, Iraq, and elsewhere (most recently in Haiti with Sudan perhaps next), are complicated.

They are complicated because of the cultural trip wires they set off and the tactical blunders that result from misunderstandings, imperial arrogance, and weak cross-cultural negotiation. Under these circumstances, security will be as temporary and fleeting in effect as whatever gain a momentary use of force may achieve.[13] Thus, even for the United States, going it alone is not a sensible geopolitical option. Nor is dictating the terms to potential partners on a take-it-or-leave-it basis much better, since it is an approach guaranteed to sideline precisely the nonaligned countries with sizeable non-Western populations who could provide those translations and offer a reassuring presence on the ground.

In this context, where the recurring threat of terror or appeals for humanitarian intervention make robust and inclusive collective action the only effective way forward, strong and effective international institutions are the only answer. Hence, there is no way around working within the UN Charter system.

AUTHORIZING FORCE:
THE ROLE OF THE SECURITY COUNCIL
AND THE LESSONS OF IRAQ

Once it became clear that the United States was unalterably determined to wage a war on terrorism on its own terms, an impending crisis for the Security Council, the United Nations, and the role of international law was clearly on the horizon. Scholars of international law cautioned that the use of the word "war" to characterize the response to the September 11 attacks could "be manipulated to provide an escape route from the constraints of international law."[14] There were extensive debates about whether the United States could apply an inherent right of self-defense under Article 51 of the UN Charter to prosecute the war against the Taliban regime. Hanging over these debates was the growing certainty that the United States would act without the sanction of international law or the authority of the Security Council.

The initial revulsion to the terror attacks of September 11, 2001, galvanized a huge global consortium of nations determined to break up terror networks and apply pressure to the states that harbored them. But once the theatre of operations shifted from Afghanistan to Iraq divisions within the Security Council turned bitter, shattering the comity of the Western Alliance, dividing NATO and as Secretary of Defense Donald Rumsfeld famously observed, separating the "Old Europe" lead by France and Germany from the "New Europe" of former Warsaw Pact countries who were committed to America's foreign policy vision. The United Nations and the broader international community faced its greatest security and diplomatic crisis since the end of the Cold War.

In a radically imperfect world of American dominance, the active threat of transnational terror groups, and no effective international political framework either in place—or imaginable in the foreseeable future—what is to be done to counter the persistent threat of terror? An instinctive revulsion to the use of force with no plan for addressing the threat would not be responsible, nor is a reading of international law that would make effective responses impossible. Nor, indeed is it in enough to offload the political and ethical responsibility onto the Security Council. Given what we know about the Security Council, that its agenda is controlled by the self-interested *realpolitik* machinations of the permanent five (P-5) veto wielding powers, we can have little confidence that ethical principles will guide decisions or effective policies will be the result. Is there a way forward out of this conundrum?

The Security Council: From Crisis to Reform?

The Security Council is deeply flawed. It operates inconsistently, sometimes fails to enforce its own resolutions, and occasionally neglects or even violates international law. It is locked into a distribution of power that privileges the veto-wielding permanent five and guarantees that dominant Western (Northern) powers will control the agenda in their own interests. An unsentimental view of the Security Council recognizes the institutional and geopolitical realities that have shaped its behavior as well as the fact that it has never assumed the autonomous authority envisioned in the UN Charter. "From the outset, the UN collective security system not only lacked the teeth of a standing UN force, but in addition the Cold War prevented the Security Council more generally from playing the role foreseen by the UN Charter," observes Niels Blokker, a international law professor and official in the Foreign Ministry of the Netherlands. "Consequently, when facing crisis situations, the member states themselves had to act, rather than rely on the UN."[15] How well can the Security Council adjust to the changed circumstances of a post-Cold War order unconstrained by competing power blocs and a post-9/11 realm of heightened, more diffuse, security threats?

Since the end of the Cold War, agreement among the five permanent members of the Security Council has been easier to achieve to paradoxical effect. On the one hand, greater consensus has revitalized the role of the Security Council in authorizing the use of force through what has come to be called "delegated enforcement action" (subcontracting and authorizing the use of force to member states). Hence, the model of delegated enforcement has been used quite routinely since 1990, not only in Iraq in 1991, but also, among other cases, in the former Yugoslavia, Somalia, Haiti, Sierra Leone, Guinnea-Bissau, and East Timor. On the other hand, as Blokker notes, "it is also clear that the role which is in fact now being played by the Council is limited to legitimizing the use of force, without keeping it under strict control."[16]

In part, the delegated use of force has come increasingly into play as the recurring horrors of humanitarian catastrophes have contributed to a sea change in perspectives about sovereignty. Indeed, since the 1990s, a widening circle of international non-governmental organizations, member states, and the last three Secretaries General have argued that a mandate to intervene in the face of gross human rights violations should trump the sovereign rights of a state to assert exclusive jurisdiction and control over anything that occurs inside its borders. In cases such as the Rwandan genocide or the ethnic cleansing in Bosnia, the United Nations was criticized for doing too little, too late, not for doing too much.[17]

For much of his term, Secretary-General Kofi Annan has labored to achieve a consensus in favor of a set of principles that would govern humanitarian intervention—and would, at the same time, enhance the authority of the Security Council by reversing the trend toward enforcement through coalitions of the willing and thereby revitalize direct Security Council control over the use of force. This would be no mean feat, since the debate over humanitarian intervention is fierce and unrelenting, pitting progressive advocates of human rights who come disproportionately from the North (the likely interveners) against the stalwart defenders of state sovereignty who come disproportionately from the South (the likely targets of humanitarian intervention).

The International Commission on Intervention and State Sovereignty (ICISS), sponsored by the Canadian government and reporting to the Secretary General in December 2001, represents a landmark effort to reconceptualize the terrain of humanitarian intervention and break this deadlock. The report was influential in devising a new conceptual framework—the "responsibility to protect"—which helped advance a productive debate that hopes to transcend North/South divisions. If the responsibility to protect is not met, then that responsibility (in accordance with strictly specified criteria) is transferred to the international community, which then has the duty to act.[18]

Understood against the backdrop of these two debates—one about the delegation of responsibilities for the Security Council's enforcement authority and the other about responsibility to protect citizens from systematic human rights abuses—the role of the Security Council in the war in Iraq comes into clearer focus.

The Disputed Lessons: Bush versus Annan

No one disagreed about the horrific human rights abuses or repressive character of the Iraqi regime, but there the agreement ended. Those supporting the Anglo-American case for war argued that member states must act when the Security Council was not able to exercise true collective security, and that Iraq represented a case where the demands of collective security in the post-9/11 world and the commitments to human rights presented mutually reenforcing arguments for military intervention. Opponents argued that the near unilateral exercise of American power against the majority will of the Security Council was spurred by a complex set of partisan, geopolitical, and economic motives, justified by unproven and misrepresented allegations about the external dangers posed by the Saddam Hussein regime. Opponents insisted then—and insist to this day—that invasion for regime change should not be confused with humanitarian intervention.

When President Bush spoke to the General Assembly on September 12, 2002, he challenged the body to "serve the purpose of its founding or become irrelevant." The administration and supporters of the war conclude that when the Security Council refused to ratify the American and British decision to go to war, the United Nations served notice of its irrelevance. However, as the international law professor Richard Falk has observed, to those who opposed the war, the Security Council "served the purpose of its founding by its refusal to endorse recourse to a war that could not be persuasively reconciled with the UN Charter and international law."[19]

There is a third option: that the failure of the Security Council to effectively assert its authority before the war in Iraq and the manifest problems of securing order and the political transition to democratic governance by a sovereign Iraq after the war, opens the door for Security Council reform. Is there a possibility that dissidents among the P-5 and a broader coalition of powerful member states mobilized by the Secretary-General might insist that the Council exert greater control over the "sub-contracted" use of force?

A year later, when President Bush returned to the United Nations for the opening session of the General Assembly in September 2003 nothing had been settled. Saddam Hussein remained at liberty (he was captured in December of that year). The pace and deadliness of the attacks in Iraq was increasing and the targets had spread from the American occupation forces to the United Nations mission in Iraq and the office of the International Red Cross. No weapons of mass destruction had been found (and by growing consensus, none of any consequence seem likely ever to be found). In fact, as military and, increasingly, civilian casualties mounted, and the prospects for stability—not to mention democracy—seemed uncertain at best, none of the justifications Bush had used to anchor his war plan were holding firm. The president's support at home was imperiled and his "my way or the highway" approach to the United Nations and the international community seemed increasingly self-defeating.

Against this backdrop, the sequence of speeches presented in turn by Kofi Annan and George Bush to the opening session of the United Nations General Assembly in September 2003 took on great importance. They reveal the stakes in this debate about the role of the Security Council, the difficulties that litter the path of reform, and the shifting fortunes of the President and the Secretary General.

Speaking first to an expectant Assembly chamber, Annan forcefully acknowledged the threats the international community faced in new forms of terror and weapons of mass destruction. He conceded that these new challenges to world

The capture of Saddam Hussein in December 2003 provided a short-lived political bounce for President Bush, but as it became clear that no weapons of mass destruction were likely to be discovered, President Bush's justifications for the invasion of Iraq began to ring hollow.

Source: Chappate, *International Herald Tribune,* August 7, 2003.

peace and security had created discord among member states about how to weigh the relative gravity of these "hard" threats against the "soft" threats of poverty, inequality, disease, and environmental degradation. Then, in the most controversial section of what many UN insiders consider Annan's defining speech as General-Secretary, Annan reproached the United States for insisting that the new context of technologically sophisticated weapons and uncontrollable terror networks have given states "the right and obligation to use force pre-emptively." Despite his mellifluous tone and diplomatic language, Annan's passionate denunciation of the U.S. strategic defense doctrine came through loud and clear. "This logic represents a fundamental challenge to the principles on which, however imperfectly, world peace and stability have rested for the last 58 years," intoned Annan. "My concern is that, if it were to be adopted, it could set precedents that resulted in a proliferation of the unilateral and lawless use of force, with or without justification."

It is interesting that despite his evident dismay with the lawlessness of the Iraqi invasion and disdain for the preemption doctrine which provided its rationale, Annan gave credence to the fears and threats that impelled America to stretch "pre-emptive war" into the realm of what has been called "preventive war."[20] Annan made clear that he rejected the right asserted by the United States to extend the doctrine of self-defense against visible and imminent attack to cover the far more contentious and potentially destabilizing right to respond to potential threats over the horizon.

At the same time, Annan acknowledged both that powerful concerns motivated the American doctrine—and that the new security threats posed a critical challenge to the United Nations system of collective security that had been developed in a now remote era. It "is not enough to denounce unilateralism, unless we face up squarely to the concerns that make some States feel uniquely vulnerable, since it is those concerns that drive them to take unilateral action," observed Annan. "We must show that those concerns can, and will, be addressed effectively through collective action.'[21] In other words, it is imperative that the Security Council urgently take up the necessary reforms that would obviate the need for states to act "pre-emptively" (in fact, the objection is to the preventive not the pre-emptive use of force) to meet the threats such as those posed by terror networks with weapons of mass destruction.

Annan challenged the world community to resolutely face the "fork in the road" and decide whether or not to scrap a system of collective authority grounded in the UN's claim to a monopoly on the legitimate use of force in the international arena. With copies of the Secretary General's remarks distributed widely in advance, and the United States looking to gain support for a Security Council resolution authorizing an American-led multinational force in Iraq, the setting was ripe for the American president to reassure the world community that it would pursue the fork of collective security. Instead of providing such reassurance, Bush reiterated his familiar defense of the war in Iraq, asserting Hussein's ties to terror networks, his prior use of weapons of mass destruction, and his refusal to account for them. "The Security Council was right to vow serious consequences if Iraq refused to comply," insisted President Bush. "And because there were consequences, because a coalition of nations acted to defend the peace, and the credibility of the United Nations, Iraq is free. . . ."[22]

Would Bush back his stated commitments with action? The President's proposal for a new antiproliferation resolution was likely to flounder in the absence of a "no first use" pledge from the United States, which Bush seemed highly unlikely to support. His renewed pledge for $15 billion over five years to meet the global AIDS crisis would mean little without the presidential leadership needed to break the logjam in Congress. Most significantly, his defense of the credibility of the United Nations itself lacked credibility. As one UN insider put it, Bush "justified the Iraq war as defending 'the peace and credibility of the United Nations,' when his administration had in fact done its best to undermine that credibility in the rush to battle."[23] If, as Kofi Annan argued, the United Nations faced a fork in the road—a stark choice between the unilateral unauthorized use of force and a system of collective security enshrined in the UN Charter—there could be little doubt that the American president was continuing to assert his hegemonic right of blank-check preemption.

America's Return to the UN: A Hollow Victory

Despite the feverish diplomatic activity between Bush's address to the General Assembly in late September and the unanimous vote by the Security Council in Resolution 1511 a few weeks later to authorize a multinational occupation of Iraq under U.S.-led coalition authority, few considered the resolution very promising. The United States (and co-sponsor Britain) conceded enough language about the UN's political role and sovereignty for the Iraqi people to bring on board key players who had opposed the war (most significantly Germany, France, and Russia) and saw nothing to be gained by another bruising schism with the United States. But the public displays of diplomatic comity could not paper over the lack of agreement regarding the most critical issues: the legitimacy of occupation, the timing of the transfer of authority to a bona fide Iraqi authority, the role and efficacy of the United Nations in peacekeeping, providing humanitarian assistance, and establishing a new democratic political order.

Little was won beyond the diplomatic victory of the unanimous passage of the resolution. One observer characterized the meager spoils of victory this way:

The White House did not seek this resolution because they felt a need for moral and legal absolution and approbation from the United Nations. It wanted it as a means to four specific goals: to coax more troop contributions from reluctant governments; to coax more cash for Iraqi reconstruction; to coax Kofi Annan to return UN civilian staff to Iraq; and perhaps most of all, reinforced by the previous three, to persuade the bulk of Iraqis that they weren't really occupied at all. It is highly unlikely to secure any of these goals.[24]

If there was any unmistakable lesson in the passage of UN Security Council Resolution 1511 it was that too little had changed from the passage of UN Security Resolution 1441, also unanimously, a little more than a sad and memorable year before, in November 2002. Resolution 1441 condemned Iraq for its "material breach" of previous UN resolutions on weaponry, human rights and terrorism, demanded "full and immediate compliance by Iraq without conditions or restrictions with its obligations" and gave Iraq "one final opportunity to comply" or face "serious consequences". Resolution 1511 provided the inter-

By the fall of 2003 America seemed stuck in Iraq, the reconstruction process stalled, and resistance to occupation intensified. Reluctantly, the United States returned to the UN to enlist international support in the reconstruction effort. But with the targets of armed attacks widening to including the UN itself and other humanitarian missions, and the United States unwilling to concede real authority to the UN, few were eager to take on the assignment.

Source: Chappate, *NZZ am Sonntag*, August 7, 2003.

national authority for the United States and United Kingdom as Coalitional Provisional Authority to conduct the occupation and configure Iraq's postwar regime largely as it sees fit to do. The UN Security Council had come full circle, moving past the deadlocks in the run up to the Iraqi invasion, to once again apply intentionally vague language to paper over critical disagreements in substance after the war exactly as it had done before the war.

Other lessons were harder to divine. Annan and Bush were clearly at loggerheads, but the exchange invited the possibility that like any wary negotiators, they were preserving room for compromise. Maybe there wasn't a fork in the road, but a lane merge around the bend. By the fall of 2003, George Bush was seeking ways to mollify detractors at home, steal the thunder from his emboldened Democratic challengers, reassure restive allies—and recruit non-American military personnel to relieve the pressure on weary American troops and financial contributions from allies to offset the whopping price tag of the ongoing Iraqi occupation.

While it was clear that President Bush would offer no apologies for the war in Iraq, it was equally clear that the administration was ratcheting down tensions with Iran and North Korea, the other members of the exclusive "axis of evil" club. Neither P-5 counterparts nor American taxpayers had to worry when the next shoe would drop, for it was quite clear that the United States was presenting unauthorized use of massive force for regime change as the exception, not the rule. It appeared for the time being—as a matter of prudence if not conviction—that Bush was putting in mothballs the doctrine of pre-emptive war that had justified the invasion of Iraq in the absence of immediate and imminent threat to the homeland.

By early 2004, the White House had executed a complete reversal in its dismissive attitude toward the United Nations in the run up to war. In fact, the Bush administration turned to the United Nations to broker an agreement to break the political deadlock over how to constitute an Iraqi transitional authority by the American deadline of June 30. By April, as the June 30 deadline for the transfer of sovereignty approached, and U.S. forces experienced mounting losses, the President seemed increasingly desperate to call in the United Nations to take as visible a role as possible in brokering a deal to put in place an interim Iraqi government by the end of June 2004. In the end, the U.S. pulled a rabbit out of UN envoy Lakhdar Brahimi's hat, as he was put under unrelenting pressure to accede to the appointment of Ayad Allawi as prime minister.

The UN was placed once more in the unenviable role of legitimizing—and helping to implement against overwhelming odds—decisions in postwar Iraq over which it had no control, decisions that gave added credibility after the fact to a war that the UN Security Council had been unwilling to endorse before the fact. Thus the pattern established with Resolution 1511 was repeated with the passage of resolution 1546 in June 2004, which formally ended Iraq's foreign occupation and endorsed the Anglo-American plan for "sovereignty-lite"—the transfer of administrative and political power in Iraq to the interim government headed by Allawi but still reliant upon and accountable to the United States.

Through the end of August 2004, the United Nations remained politically trapped in Iraq, and yet all but absent. As the new UN special representative to Iraq, Pakistan's former ambassador to Washington, Ashraf Jehangir Qazi put it, security was "not only the first consideration, it is the first priority, the second priority and the third priority" for operating a full-scale mission in Baghdad. It is important to note that the effectiveness of the United Nations in Iraq is compromised—and Annan's hands are tied—not only by the United States, but also by the unwillingness of other countries (and in particular Muslim countries) to commit forces to protect the UN mission. That may change, but unless and until it does, it will be all but impossible for the UN to meet the responsibilities accorded it by Resolution 1546, to play a leading role in securing a democratic transition by January 2005. Despite the overwhelming odds against success, it is likely to be held responsible for failure in Iraq, an outcome that would weaken the UN further for the challenges that lie ahead.

Security Council Reform: A Practical Proposal

Global attitudes against the unilateral use of force by the United States converge with America's need to off-load some of the responsibilities of occupation in Iraq and avoid the political and economic cost of comparable campaigns any time soon. In this context, as the debate about the fork in the road intensifies, Security Council reform might gain traction as the desirable result of this process of almost unwitting mutual adjustment. Concerned that the war in Iraq had "exposed deep divisions" among members of the United Nations, in September 2003 Kofi Annan announced plans to establish the High-Level Panel on Threats, Challenges and Change. Threats to peace and security were placed at the top of the panel's agenda and it seems likely that proposed reforms of the Security Council will be among the most significant—and controversial—proposals in the final report due on the Secretary-General's desk on December 1, 2004.

What are the prospects for Security Council reform? The cynicism of the United States and the P-5 dominance and balance of power politics that determine outcomes at the Security Council make reform very difficult. As a matter of course, highly partisan national interests have trumped the classic principles of collective security enshrined in the Charter which envisioned use of force initiated by the Security Council.[25] And we have to reckon with a world in which global institutions for governance and security are seldom effective or legitimate (and almost never both at the same time)—and yet predatory states and those that harbor terror networks must be deterred. Under these circumstances, as LSE international relations professor Chris Brown makes clear, "it may sometimes be necessary for nonpredatory states to act unilaterally or outside the official institutional structure."[26]

Even with the resolute advocacy of the Secretary-General marshaled to advance the U.N.'s monopoly over the legitimate use of force, and pitted against America's more manipulative use of the Security Council to provide political cover for what amounts to unilateral initiatives, reform will not be easy. Under these conditions, what options remain for the more legitimate and effective use of force to meet the post-9/11 security threats? It seemed at least possible that a consensus might emerge for a more crisply delineated standard for authorized, if delegated, use of force.

What might such an enhanced delegated enforcement model look like? As Duke University international relations specialist Robert Keohane has noted, one of the signal flaws of the existing system of delegated authority is its lack of conditionality: as it stands now, once authority is sought and authorized, too often the leaders of a potential coalition of the willing are effectively granted *carte blanche* by the Security Council. The tightening of delegated authority for the use of force, if it is to be meaningful, must narrow the discretionary powers of the contracting parties. There must be explicit agreements about the justification for military intervention, the political objectives of the campaign, and the protection of civilian populations. In addition, parties proposing military enforcement action must accept an explicit commitment to the rapid turnover of authority to a UN administration, with civil authority over the country, supported for as long as necessary by forces from the occupying powers.[27]

Prior authorization and an agreement on benchmarks such as these might be possible to achieve, precisely because they are not too sweeping. Indeed, they would reinforce the trend toward authorized coalitions of the willing, in effect formalizing and codifying the trend, and in that respect falling far short of the Secretary General's call for a renewal of the classic Charter system of collective authority for the use of force. But in a radically imperfect world where the instinctive response to security threats is national as are the military delivery systems, where international politics is conducted in and around terribly inadequate institutions for global governance, and where the rule of law is held hostage to great power politics, the opportunities for reform, although present, are limited. As Chris Brown proposes, "States should, as far as possible, try to act in such a way that they encourage the transformation of the world into one in which effective institutions do exist, or at a minimum do not make such a transformation more difficult."[28]

In this context, Annan's charge to the UN community to take the fork in the road that affirms the system of collective security implicitly overstates the prior effectiveness of a pure Charter system of collective security as distinct from an evolving use of delegated authority by the Security Council. After all, the Security Council was stymied for some 45 years by Cold War hostilities in its determination to satisfy its charter obligations to take "primary responsibility for the maintenance of international peace and security." But starting with the Middle East crisis of 1956, and especially after the ebbing of the Cold War made Security Council action more likely, its responsibilities for peace and security were increasingly met through the use of peacekeeping forces. Success has been very difficult to achieve in cases when peacekeeping operations—multinational forces operating under United Nations authority and command—were deployed in the most volatile circumstances where the conflicts raged in the absence of secure cease-fires. In such cases—for example, in Bosnia, Somalia, Rwanda, and Haiti— peacekeeping operations had to be supplemented by delegated enforcement operations under the command of single countries or a coalition of powers willing to take on the military responsibilities.[29]

Paradoxically, since there is no pure era of charter-based collective security to which to return, it may be easier to advance the path forward to a system of transparently negotiated terms for the prior authorization of the delegated use of force. This process would enhance the credibility of the UN charter and, at the same time, the broadest possible legitimacy and material support would be provided for the use of force when imminent security threats or the danger of humanitarian catastrophe warrant military intervention. For if there is any lesson that nearly everyone accepts from the war in Iraq, it is that going it alone with ambiguous and contested Security Council authority and no clear script for securing the peace reduces the prospects for success on anyone's terms. From this perspective, multilateral action authorized and controlled by the United Nations is not an ideological preference or merely one among a set of alternative options. Rather a resolute and honest effort to secure delegated, stipulated authorization from the Security Council remains the unavoidable precondition for the legal, just, and effective use of force to respond to the security threats of the post-9/11 world.

CHAPTER 6

Has 9/11 Changed Everything?
Globalization, Empire,
and the Nation-State

After the terror attacks on the World Trade Center, it was common to hear the anguished lament, "9/11 has changed everything." Certainly, the terror attacks, at a stroke, changed something very basic in American culture. The sense of national invulnerability was lost, replaced by dark fears of unknown enemy forces that reached powerfully into daily life as color-coded terror alerts raised disquieting and unfamiliar anxieties about the everyday safety of friends and family members. The sense of unrivaled and fundamentally unassailable global leadership was also lost, and with that the taken-for-granted assumption that America could draw on an inexhaustible supply of Joseph Nye's "soft power," the capacity to set the political agenda, influence individuals, nations, and states across the world by example and inspire others to emulate America because they admire its values.[1] The argument for America's soft power leadership remains powerful, but at an emotional level it will take many years to put to rest the question—"Why do they hate us?"—that sprung to the lips of so many Americans in the immediate aftermath of the terror attacks in September 2001.

Much was changed, too, in practical hard power terms. Certainly the alliance strategy and geopolitical focus of U.S. foreign policy was transformed. The Bush administration elevated the fight against terrorism to the highest national priority, and quickly assembled an extraordinarily heterodox alliance, including yesterday's Cold War nemesis, Russia, and states beginning with Pakistan, who had been treated as outcasts. Willingness to back the U.S.-led, antiterror campaign and a country's strategic importance in that campaign were the sole criteria for entry. Inevitably, other priorities (both soft and hard) were sacrificed. The need for Chinese foreign policy support on 9/11—intensified further by efforts to mitigate its objections to the war in Iraq and gain its willingness to pressure North Korea to disarm its nuclear weapons program—took human rights issues off the table.

As for Russia, after 9/11 President Vladimir Putin won tacit approval from the United States for his often-brutal campaign in Chechnya. In the aftermath of the school hostage taking and attack in Beslan, Russia, in September 2004, which resulted in the death of hundreds of children, parents, and teachers, Putin lashed out at critics in the West who urged moderation. Before the horrific hostage taking and assault, the United States had officially urged Russia to negotiate a peaceful solution to the Chechen conflict. But after Beslan, as both President Bush and President Putin equated the attacks with 9/11, the White House offered unequivocal support for Putin's hard line approach and made it clear that they would no longer second-guess Russia's refusal to negotiate with Chechen separatists.

In addition, and very noticeably, Pakistan got a "get out of jail free card" from its American-led international sanctions dating from May 1998, when (responding to Indian nuclear tests) this predominantly Muslim South Asian power, home to Taliban and Al-Qaeda minions and probably to senior leadership as well, set off a series of underground nuclear devises. The concerns about Pakistan were neither forgotten nor forgiven, but the United States nevertheless embraced this new and potentially critical "ally of convenience" within a few weeks of the terror attacks.[2] And there would be no turning back. Even the admission in February 2004 by Abdul Qadeer Khan, the "father" of Pakistan's nuclear arms program, that he had illegally sold secrets to North Korea, Libya, and Iran generated only a measured response from the White House.

In the aftermath of September 11, 2001, one couldn't help but think that the war against terrorism would define a new global epoch, but applying "before and after 9/11" as a lens for analyzing the contemporary geopolitical terrain can be risky to the extent that it distorts our understanding of how the processes of globalization have recast the capacities of states and the exercise of state power. Given the complex interplay of security threats and other dimensions of global politics, as well as the fact that we are enmeshed in the early stages of an uncertain and politically divisive antiterror campaign, it is not surprising that agreement over the role 9/11 plays in rewriting themes of globalization is extremely elusive.

Does it mark a decisive moment in the evolution of the United States as a reluctant but necessary empire, a moment when one state alone consolidated overwhelming power, achieving autonomy and exercising sovereign capacity at the expense of all others? Or, raw emotions aside, should September 11 be understood as a moment in an unending pattern of the paradoxical processes of globalization—the simultaneous strengthening and weakening of nation-states, the intensification of interdependencies and vulnerabilities, the application of global governance to peace and security punctuated intermittently by episodes of conscience-wrenching violence?

FROM DOCTRINE TO EMPIRE?

Even before the terror attack, observers were quick to note a corrosive arrogance that goes with the all too comfortable label of "the world's only superpower." For years, long before the presidency of George W. Bush there was an abiding sense in Washington, among business leaders and media opinion makers, and spreading down to Main Street and classroom America, that the United States was "doing the world a favor."[3] Yet, the willingness of the United States to exercise what Ikenberry termed "strategic restraint" lent a sense of continuity to U.S. foreign policy.

Has the 'Bush Doctrine' (for better or worse) fundamentally transformed the principles that govern American diplomacy, the most powerful country not only able but willing to advance its national interests and exert state power to secure desirable outcomes autonomously—without regard to the preferences of key allies and at the expense of their capacity to exercise power?

This view that something fundamental has changed in U.S. foreign policy— that it has jettisoned more than 50 years of strategic constraint—gained force with the appearance of an aggressive National Security Strategy in September 2002. The document crystallized Bush's signature on foreign affairs and codified the beginnings of a distinctive doctrine. It was then catapulted to the status of a dominant paradigm with the invasion of Iraq, which so vividly illustrated the doctrine and that symbolized (depending on your opinion of the war in Iraq) what was either good or bad about America's new, more aggressive and unilateralist security and geopolitical strategy. Did the emerging Bush Doctrine signal the birth of a new American Empire, made possible—supporters would say made necessary—by the terror attacks on the World Trade Center and the Pentagon?

As one observer put it simply, "Before September 11, 2001, only critics linked the United States with empire."[4] In 1992, Paul Wolfowitz, who was then under secretary of defense for policy, assisted by Lewis Libby, a relatively unknown political appointee at the Pentagon, wrote a *Defense Policy Guidance* (DPG), which set forth the case for what would ultimately be called the Bush Doctrine. It stated that the "first objective is to prevent the re-emergence of a new rival," made no mention of collective security through the United Nations, and concluded that "the United States should be postured to act independently when collective action cannot be orchestrated" through ad hoc coalitions.[5]

The paper was a blueprint for the American use of military power to advance national interests and secure a favorable global order. In short, it was the rogue version of what would come to be known as the 'Bush Doctrine' (the mission statement for the George W. Bush foreign policy agenda). But when the document was leaked to the *New York Times* shortly after its in-house circulation at the Pentagon, the then National Security Adviser, Brent Snowcroft, and Secretary of State James Baker, the foreign policy heavyweights in the George H.W. Bush administration, sent the DPG back for a drastic rewrite. Ironically, under the direction of Secretary of Defense Dick Cheney, the most controversial elements of this prescription for empire were excised, although it is clear that they were not forgotten.

Since the terror attacks, however, times have changed. In the administration of the second President Bush the authors and reluctant editors of the DPG reemerged in far more powerful positions—with Cheney routinely described as the most powerful vice president in American history, Libby serving as Cheney's chief of staff, and Wolfowitz assuming the highly influential role of Deputy Secretary of Defense.[6] In the aftermath of September 11 the *Defense Policy Guidance* was dusted off, test-marketed, and reissued as official policy, marking the first radical shift in strategic design since the advent of the Cold War. Initially tested by Bush in his West Point graduation speech in June 2002[7] and subsequently given formal status in the National Security Strategy issued in September 2002, the document argued that new dangers at the "crossroads of radicalism and technology" required a new strategic posture.[8] Was it the blueprint for a new American empire—a critical departure in American geopolitical strategy that would leave its mark on future presidents?

The National Security Strategy justified what was termed "preemption" by asserting that September 11 created a new kind of threat that could not be met by the suddenly anachronistic Cold War doctrines of deterrence and containment: "We must be prepared to stop rogue states and their terrorist clients before they are able to threaten or use weapons of mass destruction against the United States and our allies and friends."[9] But buried within the emotive rhetoric about the security dangers posed by unchecked terror networks is the classic *realpolitik* rationale for preventive war that has far less to do with the real concerns of post-9/11 security and far more to do with America's assertion of the hegemonic right to lock in the benefits of overwhelming military superiority.

Consider this excerpt from the National Security Strategy:

> The United States must and will maintain the capability to defeat any attempt by an enemy—whether a state or nonstate actor—to impose its will on the United States, our allies, or our friends. . . . Our forces will be strong enough to dissuade potential adversaries from pursuing a military build-up in hopes of surpassing, or equaling, the power of the United States.

Michael Walzer argues convincingly that perfect security is a utopian dream and that preventive war assumes a "standard against which danger is to be measured" that has nothing to do with the facts on the ground, "but exists in the mind's eye, in the idea of a balance of power," which has become the dominant idea in international relations for 300 years or more. "A preventive war is a war fought to maintain the balance of power,"[10] concludes Walzer. More than anything else the National Security Strategy should be viewed as statement of intent that the United States will no longer accept the existing balance of power.

The new defense doctrine served notice that the United States was poised to put into effect Mearsheimer's *offensive realism*. And, it would do so with a vengeance even, as in the case of the war in Iraq, where Mearsheimer parted company with the America's global strategy, arguing very publicly that the case for war was not proven and that a containment strategy was far preferable to a potentially destabilizing war.[11] Whatever else explains the war in Iraq, it can best be understood within the grand design of balance of power politics, in the shift from a hegemonic to an imperial power. At a stroke, it recast the Middle East to advance American material and geopolitical interests and signaled in the strongest possible terms the arrival of a new doctrine that no country or alliance dare challenge the overwhelming superiority of American force.

In his influential essay on European/American relations, *Of Paradise and Power*, Robert Kagan writes that American leaders should not allow themselves to be tied down by other states and, in particular, by the European Lilliputians who lack both the power and the will to limit the exercise of power by the United States.[12] If any proof that the Bush administration got the message is needed, it may be found in the diplomatic prelude to the war in Iraq, which pitted the United States against Germany and France, and in Defense Secretary Donald Rumsfeld's dismissal of these erstwhile allies as the "Old Europe."

Empire may not be pretty or diplomatic, but it has become the name of the game of America's post-9/11 geopolitical strategy and has generated a far-reaching intellectual and policy debate that has captured the popular imagination. Some observers like Michael Ignatieff have come reluctantly to accept what might be termed "empire-lite": intervention but not colonialism to advance human rights and nation-building under American leadership, preferably backed by the international community.[13] Others led by Niall Ferguson herald a new era defined by an unabashed U.S. empire, and exhort America to throw off its cultural reluctance to "do Empire" and put its best and brightest into an enduring imperial project.[14]

Still others are highly critical. Longtime antiwar critic Jonathan Schell laments the path taken by the United States since 9/11 to achieve universal empire by extending the rule of force to its logical extreme, and positioning itself to "impose America's will on nations in almost any area of their collective existence."[15] Charles Kupchan, an international relations professor and former National Security Council staffer, argues that America's dominance is rather ephemeral and that it is time for both America and the rest of the world to both contemplate now and plan for life later after Pax Americana.[16]

THREE THESES ON GLOBALIZATION AND STATE POWER

Wise or foolish, fleeting or enduring, is the "new American empire" the answer to the question that has plagued the globalization debate: what has replaced the Cold War as the defining geopolitical architecture of this era? In other words, how has Empire recast globalization and in particular the power of states: who wins when America exerts its hegemonic designs? There is no simple or single answer, but among the disparate alternatives, we have introduced and drawn insight throughout the book from three theses on globalization and state power:

1. The invisible hand
2. The contested sovereignty of the state
3. Globalization as the engine of democracy and progress.

We now develop each thesis in turn and assess their utility in answering our core interlocking questions about globalization, state power, and American hegemony.

Thesis I: The Invisible Hand

The invisible hand thesis emphasizes the compatibility of the economic goals of the American colossus and the institutional arrangements for global economic governance. It downplays the importance of grand geopolitical and military strategies, while emphasizing the dominant position that America sustains through the normal give-and-take of market forces. As Robert Hunter Wade puts it, "With whatever degree of intentionality, today's international economic architecture ensures that the ordinary operation of world market forces—the process we call globalization—tends to shore up American power by yielding disproportionate economic benefits to Americans and conferring autonomy on U.S. economic policy-makers while curbing the autonomy of all others."[17]

Thesis 1 is about the manifest benefits of the international financial architecture expressed through Adam Smith's "invisible hand" of market inputs. It is the world Thomas Friedman described with his "Electronic Herds" moving investments and currency around the world, turning on a dime to find short-term advantages, and state leaders with their hats in hand trying to attract foreign investment. And in this world, the benefits of economic hegemony are widespread and significant.

They include the sphere of maneuver accorded by the function of the dollar as the primary currency for trade, foreign exchange reserves, and currently speculation. Hence, America can exert unique influences on exchange rates and interest rates throughout the world to advance domestic policy goals such as boosting growth, reducing unemployment, and protecting domestic companies from competition. Economic hegemony also means that the United States can tolerate substantial trade deficits, due to the self-interested cooperation of trade surplus countries, in East Asia and elsewhere, to maintain very substantial dollar holdings.

As another benefit of its dominant international position, as Stiglitz argues, the United States gains the most from the rules that govern the workings of key institutions of global economic governance such as the WTO and the IMF. These international institutions extend the legitimacy of multilateral organizations to bail out policies that reduce the risk of defaults that would hurt American financial institutions. In addition, they promulgate trade and development agreements that advantage the global reach of American high-technology sectors, even as they permit the protection of politically influential U.S. companies in districts which are considered critical to the electoral success of the governing party.

According to Thesis 1, theories of globalization that emphasize technological innovation, the shrinking of time and space, the natural expansion and anarchic vitality of capital markets, and the global diffusion of opportunities, miss the critical linkage between globalization, empire, and state power. Wade argues, "This is the paradox of economic globalization—it looks like 'powerless' expansion of markets but it works to enhance the ability of the United States to harness the rest of the world and fortify its empire-like policy."[18]

Hence, the current global dominance of the United States reveals hegemony in all its glory: America enjoys a dominant position in the global economic balance of power, which appears natural and inevitable in a world where American values of competitiveness, free markets, and neoliberal states prevail.[19] The direct military exercise of power follows from the economic dominance, a proposition that defines the core argument of the first thesis on globalization, empire, and state power.

Thesis 1: The Invisible Hand. *The economic advantages of hegemony make empire, defined by overwhelming military superiority and dominant economic and geopolitical power, possible. The aims and rules of the contemporary global geopolitical and economic architecture—whether by design, the near-universal appeal and adoption of American market-based values, or the "invisible" hand of market forces—sustain the dominance of the United States in economic and geopolitical terms. The framework of the Washington Consensus institutions also makes possible American military superiority and to an important degree motivates the unilateral use of force to secure strategic goals. Hence globalization is best understood as a process that sustains American power at the expense of all other nation-states.*

Thesis 2: The Contested Sovereignty of the State Thesis

In the first wave of enthusiasm for globalization, some observers were quick to argue that the radical mobility of factors of production had effectively swamped the capacities of the nation-state. For example, Kenichi Ohmae, proclaiming the end of the nation-state, argued that the "information-led transition to a gen-uinely borderless economy" raised troubling questions about the relevance—and effectiveness—of nation-states as meaningful units in terms of which to think about, much less manage, economic activity.[20]

Of course, there is a kernel of truth to this argument. Any account of global-ization in the contemporary period must take on board the neoliberal bias of the global economy. States must and do operate within the constraints of competitive pressures for global market share in key sectors, which tend to reward those who encumber inward foreign investment the least. Likewise competition (as well as political bargains over deficits struck in the European Union) weakens the capac-ity of states to provide social protections for their citizens. In addition, as Stiglitz demonstrates, the policies set by key institutions such as the WTO and the IMF enforce this neo-liberal bias through a persistent system of reward and punish-ment that disciplines the behavior of nation-states in the developing world. And, as we have seen, a fairly crude interpretation of globalization has captured the popular imagination through the writing of Thomas Friedman and others, who claim that globalization leaves no choice for national leaders but to don the "Golden Straightjacket" and sing the mantra of free trade, austerity in social programs, democratic reform, and minimal deficits.

Thesis 2, however, insists that reports about the demise of the nation-state are premature. As we saw in Part 1, Germany is not Britain when it comes to economic and social models and competitiveness and Taiwan is not Korea when the underlying story of alternate strategies and differential state capacities for meeting the Asian economic crisis came into focus. The resilience and strength of the state are also revealed by the workings of institutions of global governance— from the WTO to the EU—which are driven by the highly partisan national agendas of the most powerful members. It is not only in Afghanistan or Iraq, but also in EU summits and WTO ministerials that "coalitions of the willing" come together to advance global agendas through concerted state action.

As effectively as anyone, sociologist Michael Mann has advanced the core principles of Thesis 2 on the relationship between globalization, the state, and the new American empire. Mann finds the eagerness of many observers of global-ization to claim that the state has been weakened or transcended confounding. In fact, both the omnipresence of states (there are now some 200) and the intensifi-cation of interstate negotiations over the economy, the environment, and war and peace are part and parcel of globalization. As Mann observes:

> *This makes globalisation not only transnational (breaking through the boundaries of states), but also inter-national (concerning the relations between states). Globalisation does not sweep away national, regional or other local differences, but it partly operates through them. So globalisation is not unitary but multiple; it concerns states; and it inevitably generates conflict.*[21]

According to Thesis 2, globalization and state power is explained best by close empirical study of the processes of multi-level governance and the play of forces shaped by a volatile mix of transnational and international politics. Globalization does not adhere to a linear trajectory: states matter, outcomes differ, and trend lines are illusory. Globalization is always pregnant with its opposite: it hastens both development and exclusion from development; it makes some states weaker and others stronger. Globalization makes 9/11 possible but also creates the potential for collective responses to disable international terror networks. Globalization creates the conditions (discussed in Thesis 1) for the emergence of the United States as the first new empire of the twenty-first century, but provides no guarantees that it can control outcomes, maintain its preeminent status, or prevent a countervailing power from emerging. In fact, according to this thesis, the United States is privileged and dominant in the era of globalization, but it is neither all powerful nor immune from the constraints imposed by multi-level governance and contested sovereignty.

Thesis 2: The Contested Sovereignty of the State. *Globalization does not mark the demise of the state, but it does transform the context in which it operates. Taken together, multi-level governance, transnational processes, and international politics reduce the autonomous capacity of states to control outcomes and vastly complicate domestic politics. Globalization generates both conflict and the means for negotiating conflict; it creates institutions for global governance which operate through the prism of national politics and whose policy outcomes reflect the interstate balance of power of their members. Multi-level governance in every realm of geopolitics increases the challenges that must be faced by the United States as a hegemonic power and raises doubts about America's effectiveness or potential longevity as the first empire of the twenty-first century.*

Thesis 3: Globalization as the Engine of Democracy and Progress

Of our three theses on globalization, the state, and empire, Thesis 3 is undoubtedly the one with the greatest mainstream currency in America, and hence it is the most easily explained. The globalization as the engine of democracy and progress thesis seems to resonate with American culture and common sense. It gains additional strength from its capacity to carve out a healthy chunk of common ground from some erstwhile antagonists in the globalization and new American empire debates.

When Samuel Huntington writes, "Conflicts between the West and Islam . . . focus less on territory than on broader intercivilizational issues such as . . . human rights and democracy, control of oil, migration, Islamist terrorism, and Western intervention,"[22] he is making the case that a vast part of the world has been left behind by the processes of modernization. It is a territory trapped in an Islamic culture, cut off from the advantages of Western intervention which (in Huntington's view) brings political vitality and healthy prospects for progress toward democratic politics as well as economic development.[23] In Friedman's terminology, it is the claim that in the Middle East the healthy balance between the Lexus and the olive tree is absent, with dangerous consequences flowing from excessive attachments to tradition, nation, and culture as they are refracted through and distorted by the Arab-Israeli conflict. As a result, the benefits of globalization, modernization, and democratization are held at bay, middle-class aspirations are quashed, and traditional authoritarian regimes are propped up.

As we discussed in Chapter 1, Huntington and Friedman look at geopolitical prospects very differently, disagreeing strenuously about whether the world is retreating into tribalism or advancing to new heights through the inexorable diffusion of new technologies and the market logic of the "globalization system." But they both subscribe to Thesis 3 insofar that they assume, as they very clearly do, that the modernizing processes cultivated by Western (Northern) countries, cultures, market practices, and capacities for both political and technological innovation drive history. Equally significant, these two apparently disjunctive interlocutors in the great globalization debate undoubtedly share the commonplace view that the deficiencies in the cultural and political capital of the Arab and Muslim world make the Middle East the last to join the globalized world and the most antithetical to progress. In Friedman's usage, it is where "longitudes and attitudes" come together to help explain 9/11; a claim for which Huntington's *The Clash of Civilizations* provides the perfect preview. As one observer noted, they both "see the North as embodying rationality, progress, the future, while the South clings to 'tradition' or nurtures unreason."[24]

It is easy to see that the association of globalization with democracy and progress also provides a common touchstone for a range of otherwise somewhat disparate views in the burgeoning debate about the new American empire. Not surprisingly, an empire enthusiast such as Niall Ferguson makes no bones about the political, economic, and moral advantages that flow to the colonized:

> *The British Empire has had a pretty lousy press from a generation of "post-colonial" historians anachronistically affronted by racism. But the reality is that the British were significantly more successful at establishing market economies, the rule of law and the transition to representative government than the majority of postcolonial governments have been. The policy "mix" favored by Victorian imperialists reads like something just published by the International Monetary Fund, if not the World bank: free trade, balanced budgets, sound money, the common law, incorrupt administration and investment in infrastructure financed by international loans.[25]*

Ferguson concludes on a decidedly uncritical note that the only real problem with the emerging U.S. empire is uncertainty about America's "stamina" to see things through. "These are precisely the things Iraq needs now," observes Ferguson, hearkening back to the virtuous circle of Victorian imperialism and IMF structural adjustment programs without even a nod to the critics. "If the scary-sounding 'American empire' can deliver them, then I'm all for it."[26]

Michael Ignatieff seems more tentative and qualified in tendering his support for the advantages of Pax Americana, yet he too sees no choice but to endorse a version, albeit a more multilateralist version, of the new American empire. For, in the end, despite misgivings (after all he was a participant in the "Responsibility to Protect" commission which sought to confirm the central authority of the United Nations), Ignatieff has been won over. He seems persuaded by the benefits overseas interventions bring both to the presidents who take little heed of the risks of failure and keep "throwing the interventionist dice"[27] and to those in need of humanitarian intervention.

Americans tend to back presidents on global interventions, argues Ignatieff, even when the cost in lives as well as the financial costs rise, and he insists that the incessant demands for American intervention to prosecute the war on terror or to alleviate human suffering will not abate. Ignatieff struggles in his writing to find "a way out of this mess of interventionist policy" in the creation of "an international doctrine that promotes and protects [America's] interests and those of the rest of the international community."[28] In this vein he calls for quite drastic steps to reform the Security Council (including expanding the membership and eliminating veto rights) and then calls on the United States to commit to using force only with Council approval or when U.S. security is directly threatened.

But, in the end, Ignatieff seems to buckle under the sheer force of American power to embrace, if only as a last resort, the new American empire. Without a revitalized United Nations, concludes Ignatieff, the alternative is an ungainly version of empire, "a muddled, lurching America policing an ever more resistant world alone, with former allies sabotaging it at every turn."[29] But he sees the possibility (of course, not the certainty) of a renewed UN mandate, new rules for the use of force and for humanitarian intervention, and a United States committed to abide by the dictates of the international community.

The result would be a more effective and popular empire, but an empire nonetheless. As Ignatieff puts it, "A new charter on intervention would put America back where it belongs, as the leader of the international community instead of the deeply resented behemoth lurking offstage."[30] With a new mandate for leadership and renewed authority the benefits of greater stability, the establishment of democracy, and a global up tick in human rights would be all but sure to follow.

Finally, with no qualms or reservations, the globalization as engine of democracy thesis has found powerful voice in President Bush's major policy address to the National Endowment for Democracy in November, 2003, which gave new seriousness and depth to his rationale for the Iraqi invasion, casting it as a watershed moment in the "global democratic revolution."[31] Beyond that, in what *New York Times* columnist William Safire called the speech which "clearly articulated the policy . . . Bush will be remembered for,"[32] the president presented a detailed and evocative account of the advance of freedom and democracy through the expansion of markets, free enterprise, the growth of a middle-class, and "the power of instant communications to spread the truth, the news, and courage across borders."[33] In one of the most evocative passages, Bush clearly enunciated his ultimate justification for the war in Iraq:

> *Our commitment to democracy is . . . tested in the Middle East, which is my focus today, and must be a focus of American policy for decades to come. In many nations of the Middle East—countries of great strategic importance—democracy has not yet taken root. And the questions arise: Are the peoples of the Middle East somehow beyond the reach of liberty? Are millions of men and women and children condemned by history or culture to live in despotism? Are they alone never to know freedom, and never even to have a choice in the matter? I, for one, do not believe it. I believe every person has the ability and the right to be free. . . .*[34]

The speech was a spirited defense of the war in Iraq on the grounds that regime change there would lead to democratic reforms throughout the region. In short, like President Clinton, Tony Blair, and many world leaders before him, George Bush asserted the causal connection between globalization and democracy, providing a fitting capstone to our third thesis on globalization, empire, and the nation-state.

Thesis 3: Globalization as the Engine of Democracy and Progress. *Globalization spurs the diffusion of market forces, expands the size, and increases the influence of an increasingly cross-border and entrepreneurial middle class, which is increasingly committed to democratic governing structures and open economies. In mutually reinforcing patterns, the intensification of cross-border market practices, the cultural diffusion of Western (Northern) values, and the spread of new communication technologies erode the stultifying force of local cultures and challenge the authoritarian regimes in the Middle East, in particular, and throughout the world. As forceful advocate of free trade and democratic regime change, the new American empire serves as guarantor of a global order increasingly recast in its image—and serves notice on all challengers that it will do whatever may be necessary to preserve and advance the geopolitical order defined by globalization, democratization, and American hegemony.*

Each thesis provides a clear answer to our two central questions:

1. How does globalization (and in particular, the global challenges of economic competitiveness, geopolitical influence, and security from terror

attacks) affect state power understood as the capacity of states to secure desirable outcomes and influence the behavior of other states, transnational actors, and international organizations?

2. What are the consequences of America's exercise of hegemonic power—for the capacity of other states to exercise power, for the shape of the geopolitical order, and for the United States itself?

In addressing the questions that have animated this study, each thesis offers a distinctive way to integrate the findings in the three case studies (the United States, EU Europe, and East Asia) and each provides a perspective on global politics post-9/11. Each thesis makes a powerful contribution to a debate about globalization and state power and each gives rise to a particular interpretation of the consequences of America's exercise of unrivaled global power. None covers everything we would want to know about globalization and state power—and none slams the door on all the other interpretations.

Hence, we can evaluate each thesis on the strength of its empirical claims and its explanatory scope and power—but there is something more at play. For each thesis—implicitly or explicitly—expresses a mindset about America's role in the world. Each stakes a claim about proper or improper motives and about the legitimate or illegitimate exercise of state power and the use of force. Each invokes a broad moral vision both about America's role in the world and about the consequences of globalization for the fate of citizens—and the prospects of development and both material and physical security—around the world. In the end, each lays claim to a set of values and preferences that go beyond accounts of the way the world of global politics and state power works in order to assert claims about how it ought to work.

Thesis 1 (The Invisible Hand) explains that the United States is the big winner in economic globalization. It gains the most from the designs and policy aims of the international financial institutions. How could it not and preserve its standing as hegemonic power? Historically, in the post-World War II period, as Ikenberry argues, the United States had the military and geopolitical wherewithal as well as the vision to consolidate a postwar order that shaped the key institutions of global governance to advance its purpose. A doctrine of strategic restraint made a virtue of necessity, as allies and trading partners accepted the terms of two postwar settlements—a containment order and a liberal democratic order—designed by the United States but presented as the natural consequences of market forces and the inevitable demands of security. This international regime has guaranteed American dominance and, as Wade argued, conferred the legitimacy of multilateralism to a global order that advances America's state power at the expense of all other states.

Stiglitz's critique of U.S. dominance of the WTO and the IMF in response to the Asian economic crisis both brings the account up to date and draws attention to the damaging—and highly visible—consequences of international governance on American terms. America's capacity to maintain high levels of growth and cutting-edge competitiveness despite very sizeable trade and budget deficits and weak steering capacity lends additional credence to the argument that the global economic architecture locks-in advantages for the United States—and that its unrivaled geopolitical power makes it all but certain that China (and others) are willing to make the most of their symbiotic relationship with the United States, trading economic support for geopolitical advantage.

Recall, too, that according to Thesis 1, America's economic preeminence makes possible its unrivaled geopolitical power and in turn motivates American willingness to use force on its own terms, with or without the endorsement of the Security Council. America's willingness to knock heads together on the Security Council in the run up to the war in Iraq, its willingness to manipulate differences among EU countries (Old versus New Europe; Britain and Spain versus France and Germany), and its willingness to blow hot and cold and force the United Nations to do its bidding in postwar Iraq all give added weight to Thesis 1.

That said, like all claims based on the architecture and built-in design features of a set of institutions—what is often called a structural explanation—Thesis 1 has a limited capacity to explain variation in behavior and change over time. Importantly, it can not easily explain the shift from strategic restraint to the Bush Doctrine or predict what framework for U.S. foreign policy might emerge in the future. In addition, Thesis 1 does not lend itself easily to falsification. Adherents are inclined to see the United States pulling the strings and manipulating other players in the system all the time and everywhere. Ignoring the United Nations in Iraq shows American power at the expense of all other states; appealing to the United Nations shows manipulation and the abuse of power, not genuine multilateralism.

With Thesis 1, it should also be noted that there is an ambiguity in the "invisible hand" assertion. It leaves open to different conclusions the important question of the degree to which the consolidation of the postwar geopolitical and economic architecture was by American design and influence and the degree to which it was the "invisible hand" result of a confluence of market forces and geopolitical circumstances. There is also an opening to alternative judgments about winners and losers. Friedman sees near-universal advantages flowing from a system that underwrites American dominance, while Stiglitz sees systematic abuse of power by the United States (and other great powers) both directly and through their hypocritical manipulation of key global institutions to do their bidding.

Although Friedman would demur (and many readers may agree), I think the bulk of the evidence presented in this book to support Thesis 1 confirms the claim that globalization sustains American power at the expense of all other nation-states and makes it possible for the United States to bend the geopolitical order to its will. Many who read the evidence this way and, moreover, come to consider Thesis 1 the strongest contender are likely to go a step further. They will be critical of America's role in the world and concerned about a global agenda that can be controlled by any country at the expense of all others. And they will have a clear answer to the question, "Who wins when America rules?": perhaps American interests will prevail, but no one wins.

Thesis 2 (The Contested Sovereignty of the State) debunks the popular wisdom that sees globalization as the great leveler in the service of economic markets, knocking down all national differences in social policy preferences and economic models in its wake, as Friedman put it, reducing all political choices to Pepsi or Coke. According to this thesis, globalization doesn't transcend the state so much as it operates through the state, limiting its sphere of autonomous control over policy outcomes, but intensifying the role of the state in negotiating international and transnational regimes that increasingly reach into every area of everyday political life. State sovereignty is contested in the post-9/11 era of heightened concerns about security threats as it is perpetually tested in trade or environmental policy.

More powerful states—and their citizens—compete on favorable terms, but it is never easy to beat the odds, and the house gets to cut the cards. Besides, there is no free pass. The United States, as hegemonic power and putative empire, operates within the same institutional entanglements, but with a far greater range of motion: the threads don't bind Gulliver as they would the six-inch Lilliputians. But these days, Gulliver cannot break free without considerable cost. Witness the battering the United States has taken in trade disputes with Europe and the about face President Bush took in his attitude towards the United Nations a year after "Mission Accomplished" was declared in Iraq. The hegemon operates unilaterally at its peril, as the resistance to American occupation, the bloody internecine struggles that greeted the installation of the Interim Iraqi government, and the insurgent attacks on American and Iraqi security forces all confirm.

Thesis 2 is less sweeping in scope than either Thesis 1 or Thesis 3 and tends to offer more qualified judgments about globalization and state power. The strength of Thesis 2 lies in its focus on the stock-in-trade of comparative politics: state and multi-level institutions and processes; the importance and consequences of alternative economic and social models and strategies; differences in the capacity of states to respond effectively to external shocks and changing environments.

Do you see in the processes of globalization above all a changed political context, one in which states matter as much as they ever did before, but in which statecraft has been transformed by multi-level governance and the incessant demands of negotiated sovereignty? If so, Thesis 2 (Contested Sovereignty of the State) will help identify the pattern that emerges as particular states and issue areas come into view. It will help reveal how and why globalization strengthens some states (in some policy realms) and weakens others (in the same or in different ways). It will make clear that the pattern of winners and losers corresponds broadly to North/South divisions, but will also capture vividly the exceptions to this rule. Since the thesis of contested sovereignty applies to all states, including the hegemonic or imperial power, it will also shed a different light on the empire debate, supporting an analysis that sees a multipolar order potentially reasserting itself against the American colossus.

How does globalization affect state power? The vulnerabilities experienced by the United States—in trade deficits, its dependence on big-surplus countries to fund its budget deficit, and its subjection to WTO rulings—all confirm that globalization limits the capacity of any state to secure desirable outcomes and shape the behavior of other states and international organizations. The pooling of sovereignty at the heart of the EU agenda represents an historic recognition that individual states no longer have enough autonomous capacity to make a go of it in this era of globalization. The EU also represents the hope that a new form of multi-level government can meet the challenges of globalization and maximize European economic competitiveness and geopolitical clout.

Comparative analysis of the Asian economic crisis, in particular, the Korea-Taiwan comparison, demonstrates that state capacity matters when external shocks require resolute and strategically effective responses. In response to 9/11, and a new world order marked by terror, war, and instability, the United States has asserted the right to exercise power autonomously in going to war, but appears more willing in the aftermath of the war in Iraq to recognize that it cannot go it alone in consolidating the peace. To a considerable degree, it can shape the geopolitical order and use its power and influence to blunt the exercise of power by other states, but it must still rely on other states to achieve desirable collective outcomes.

Thesis 2 affirms that states matter, and asserts that national cultures, values, and institutions are the life-blood of politics. In an age of globalization—and with a mix of practical insight and moral concern— those drawn to Thesis 2 will rally to defend the importance and centrality of the nation-state as the polity that still delivers the goods to its citizens and best represents their interests and preferences in multi-level, transnational, and international contexts.

Many advocates of Thesis 2 will claim that we are in an age better defined by multi-level governance than by globalization or American hegemony. Who wins when America rules? I think that most who choose Thesis 2 as the best analytical framework will insist that no hegemonic power ever really rules alone. Many will go a step further and argue that America's exercise of hegemonic power should not be permitted to recast the geopolitical order in its image or undermine the capacity of other states to also exercise power and to govern on behalf of their citizens.

Despite expanding development gaps and deepening security threats, Thesis 3 (Globalization as the Engine of Democracy and Progress) with its reassuring vision of a safer, more prosperous, more democratic world tomorrow holds tremendous appeal. Nor is its appeal due simply to wishful or uncritical thinking. This thesis is anchored in the waves of democratic transitions that have transformed national politics in Southern Europe, Latin America, East Asia, Eastern and Central Europe, and Africa in the last 30 years. It builds on the expectations that authoritarian holdouts in every continent, especially the Middle East, will either succumb to U.S. pressure (if and when it is applied) or be drawn to democratic reform by the lure of the benefits of globalization that are thought to flow to those who accept the norms of the "Golden Straightjacket." It is not just intellectual or political elites, but huge masses of ordinary citizens around the world who are drawn to Thesis 3.

We have said that that each thesis provides an answer to our core questions about how globalization affects state power and about the consequences of America's exercise of state power; that each offers a distinctive way to integrate the findings in our three case studies; and that each also reveals and advances a particular mindset about America's role in the world and a perspective about the proper and improper exercise of state power and recourse to the use of force. In sum: each thesis rests on empirical claims and each invokes—and implicitly or explicitly seeks to advance—an ethical claim about how the world should work. How well does Thesis 3 meet these tests?

Recently, an authoritative study of comparative democracy affirmed the near-universal appeal of democratic principles and their compatibility with diverse cultural and religious traditions. But it concluded, nonetheless, that democratic societies have increasingly diverged in recent years in the quality and depth of their democracies, that the consolidation of new democracies has been problematic, and that the trend toward the expansion of democracies in the 1980s and the early 1990s has halted, at least for the time being.[35] Hence the evidence in support of Thesis 3 is not all its supporters might wish for.

In addition, consider the prospects of regime change through U.S. military intervention leading to a consolidated democracy. A recent study sponsored by the Carnegie Endowment for International Peace found that of the 16 attempts over the past century only 4 were successful—and none of the successes occurred outside the developed world and Latin America.[36] Nor does the chaos in Iraq—where the Shi'a majority has no stake in secularism, the Sunni minority rejects one-person-one-vote, and the Kurds cannot abide simple majority rule and threaten to withdraw from the national government—provide any reason to be optimistic about a democratic settlement, much less a consolidation. And of course, given the dug-in stalemate in Israeli-Palestinian relations and the pervasiveness of authoritarian regimes in the Middle East, the prospects for a democratic transformation in the region find little empirical support.

Yet, as bleak as this picture looks, there is growing evidence that the Muslim world has begun a process of change and experimentation with political models that attempt to balance the competing demands of religion and secularism in an effort to foster moderation, stability and modernization.[37] So perhaps globalization will contribute to the development of a distinctive homegrown model of government in the Muslim world, which has at least some of the attributes of democracy.

Most who favor Thesis 3 are likely to say that everyone wins when America rules, because the ethos and material and diplomatic support the United States provides advance the prospects of development and democracy. But, we think it is fair to say that the gap between the empirical claims and the ethical propositions contained in Thesis 3 are the greatest and, as a result, the Globalization as the Engine of Democracy and Progress thesis is the most contentious. Ten years ago the momentum for democratic change captured the imagination because there was confirming evidence on the ground in country after country in both the North and the South. Today, democracy, in a variety of regional and cultural versions remains unrivaled as a model of governance but the momentum for change appears to have slowed. At this historical juncture, Thesis 3 stands as a morally powerful rallying cry in search of renewed empirical confirmation, which future developments may provide.

No one thesis explains everything there is to know about globalization and state power and none fully satisfies everyone's exacting tests of empirical validation and moral conviction. But each provides a powerful point of departure for informed, reasoned, and even passionate debate about one of the most challenging themes of our era—how globalization shapes the behavior and capacity of states throughout the world and how America's unrivaled power changes the equation.

There is a profound struggle under way in America about foreign and security policy, the use of force, the terms of engagement with allies and international organizations—in short, about the exercise of state power in the post-9/11 world.[38] With the re-election of President Bush, the debate is likely to continue, even perhaps intensify. But will there be any tangible effects?

No American president will forswear the advantages of Thesis 1 (The Invisible Hand), which sustains American economic dominance. Nor is Bush likely to qualify Thesis 3 (Globalization as the Engine of Democracy and Progress) by acknowledging the intractable problems associated with the consolidation of democracies, especially in institutionally weak states or those facing huge deficits in democratic legitimacy. Any concession to the empirical weakness of the assertions contained in Thesis 3 would erode his core normative claims about America's role in the world and invite further challenge to the Bush Doctrine's vision of the proper use of force and the exercise of state power in the post-9/11 world.

Before the election many observers thought little would change with the result: a Kerry administration would neither magically resolve differences with allies and trading partners nor reduce the economic vulnerabilities that America faced. It stands to reason, therefore, that a second Bush administration, its hand strengthened by victory and expanded control of both the House and the Senate, will dig in and stay the course. That said, there is a chance that the common-sense logic of Thesis 2 (The Contested Sovereignty of the State), focused acutely by economic vulnerabilities and the enormous challenges America faces in stabilizing Iraq, might shift the administration's mindset just enough for it to reconsider the costs of how it operates as the unrivaled superpower. It is by no means clear if—or when—the United States will come to regard the strategic use of multi-level governance and a collaborative approach to multilateral institutions as a more effective way to achieve desirable outcomes. But this much is clear, if policy circles in Washington start taking seriously the implications of contested sovereignty and the perils of unilateralism for countries great and small, such thinking would go a long way toward changing the equation about globalization, state power, and the consequences of American rule.

Bibliographic Note

The data used in the figures in Chapter 1 and in the Global Profiles that appear in the book are drawn from an extensive set of sources. In nearly all cases, multiple sources were used to ensure accuracy and strenuous efforts were made to generate comparability of data.

General sources of data:

- UNESCO Year Book World Culture Report 2000, UNESCO
- World Refugee Survey (Year Book of Labor Statistics)
- International Trade Statistics (by country)
- Commodity Trade Statistics (by commodity)
- World Fact Book 2002
- OECD reports—major donors to ODA
- CD-ROM: World Development Indicators 2000, 2002

E-resources:

- *Tagish* (http://www.tagish.co.uk/) Tagish > Essential Lists > Worldwide Embassies
- CIA World Factbook 2002 (http://www.cia.gov/cia/publications/factbook/index.html)

For Economic Integration:

- The World Development Indicators CD-ROM 2002, published by the World Bank

For Information Flows:

- World Culture Report 2000, UNESCO

Table 19: Cultural Trade and Communication Trends: Communication

For People Flows:

- World Culture Report 2000, UNESCO 2000

Table 25: Cultural Context: Tertiary Education Abroad

For Political Integration:

- *Tagish* (http://www.tagish.co.uk/)
- The Convention and Kyoto Protocol (http://unfccc.int/resource/convkp.html)
- The Europa World Year Book 2002, vol. 1, Europa Publications, London and NY, 2002
- The Convention on the Elimination of All Forms of Discrimination against Women (http://www.un.org/womenwatch/daw/cedaw/)

For Cultural Influences:

- World Culture Report 2000, UNESCO 2000

  Table 6: Cultural Practices and Heritage: leading languages
  Table 4: Cultural Activities and Trends: Cinema and Film

For Security and Military Interaction:

- The World Development Indicators CD-ROM 2002, published by the World Bank (to ensure comparability 1999 data were used)

For World Indicators:

- The World Development Indicators CD-ROM 2002, The World Bank, 2002
- The Europa World Year Book 2002, vol. 1, Europa Publications, London and NY, 2002

Notes

PREFACE

[1]John Baylis and Steve Smith, eds., *The Globalization of World Politics,* 2nd ed. (Oxford: Oxford University Press, 2001), p. 7.

[2]This core definition of globalization draws on the extensive and influential work of David Held and his colleagues. See, for example: David Held, et al., *Global Transformations: Politics, Economics, and Culture* (Stanford, Ca.: Stanford University Press, 1999), pp. 27–28; David Held and Anthony McGrew, *Globalization/Anti-Globalization* (Cambridge: Polity Press, 2002), p. 1.

[3]The term "hard power" (which refers to military capability and economic strength) as well as "soft power" (which refers to the influence associated with culture and values) is drawn from the work of Joseph S. Nye. Nye argues that even in the post-9/11 era, soft power is an essential—even an increasing—component of American power, an argument to which we will return in Chapter 6. See Joseph S. Nye Jr., *The Paradox of American Power: Why the World's Only Superpower Can't Go it Alone* (New York, Oxford University Press: 2002); *Soft Power: The Means to Success in World Politics* (New York, Public Affairs: 2004).

CHAPTER I

[1]Robert F. Worth, "In New York Tickets, Ghana Sees Orderly City," *New York Times,* July 22, 2002, p. A1.

[2]"Indian Exporters Vow to Fight U.S. Rice Patent" (http://www.poptel.org.uk/panap/archives/basmati.htm) accessed on 1/13/03.

[3]M. R. Subramani, "US opposes EU move to protect basmati rice," Business Line, Internet Edition (http://www.blonnet.com/bline/2002/10/08/stories/2002100801311100.htm) accessed on 1/13/03.

[4]"James Bond is public enemy number one for Koreans," *Guardian Unlimited,* January 3, 2003 (http://film.guardian/co.uk/news/story/ 0,12589,868313,00.html).

[5]Nicholas D. Kristof, "Tunneling Toward Disaster," *New York Times,* January 21, 2003, p. A23.

[6]Richard Waters, "Apple's iPod sales overtake computers," *Financial Times,* April 15, 2004, p. 19.

[7]E. P. Thompson, *The Making of the English Working Class* (New York: Vintage, 1966), p. 198.

[8]Benedict Anderson, *Imagined Communities: reflections on the Origin and Spread of Nationalism* (London and New York: Verso, 1991).

[9]Walker Connor, "A Nation is a Nation, is a State, is an Ethnic Group, is a . . . ," in John Hutchinson and Anthony D. Smith, eds., *Nationalism* (Oxford and New York: Oxford University Press, 1994) p. 39.

[10]See Saskia Sassen, *Globalization and Its Discontents* (New York: The New Press, 1998).

[11]See David Held, *Democracy and the Global Order: From the Modern State to Cosmopolitan Governance* (Stanford, Calif.: Stanford University Press, 1995), pp. 77–83.

[12]See Stephen D. Krasner, *Sovereignty: Organized Hypocrisy* (Princeton, New Jersey: Princeton University Press, 1999), ch 1.

[13]Saskia Sassen, *Globalization and Its Discontents* (New York: The New Press, 1998), p. 92.

[14]See Richard Falk, "Sovereignty" in Joel Krieger, ed., *The Oxford Companion to Politics of the World,* 2nd ed., (New York: Oxford University Press), pp. 789–791.

[15]Lisbet Hooghe and Gary Marks, "Unraveling the Central State, but How? Types of Multi-level Governance," *American Political Science Review* Vol. 97, No. 2 (May 2003), pp. 233–243.

[16]See Susan Starnge, *The Retreat of the States: The Diffusion of Power in the World Economy* (Cambridge: Cambridge University Press , 2000), p. 3.

[17]See, for example, Kenichi Ohmae, *The End of the Nation State* (New York: Free Press, 1995), p. viii.

[18]Peter Gourevitch, *Politics in Hard Times* (Ithaca and London: Cornell University Press, 1986), pp. 35–68.

[19]Alexander Wendt, *Social Theory of International Politics* (Cambridge: Cambridge University Press, 1999), p. 9.

[20]Thomas Friedman, *The Lexus and the Olive Tree* (New York: Farrar, Straus and Giroux, 1999), p. 11.

[21]Thomas L. Friedman, *Longitudes and Attitudes: Exploring the World After September 11* (New York: Farrar, Straus, Giroux, 2002).

[22]Friedman, *Longitudes and Attitudes,* p. ix.

[23]Friedman, *The Lexus and the Olive Tree* (2001), p. 31.

[24]Friedman, *Longitudes and Attitudes*, p. 238.

[25]Thomas L. Friedman, "War of Ideas, Part 5," *New York Times,* January 22, 2004, p. A5.

[26]Samuel Huntington, *The Clash of Civilizations and the Remaking of World Order* (New York: Simon and Schuster/Touchstone, 1997), p. 21.

[27]Huntington, p. 307.

[28]Friedman, *The Lexus and the Olive Tree* (1999), p. xvii.

[29]Joseph P. Stiglitz, *Globalization and Its Discontents* (New York: Norton, 2002), p. 9.

[30]Stiglitz, p. 6.

[31]The "Group of 7" (G7) refers to high stakes economic diplomacy among the United States, Japan, Germany, Britain, France, Italy and Canada. The coordinated effort of these powerful countries with dominant economies to shape policies of the International Monetary Fund (IMF) and coordinate efforts to deal with a host of economic and geopolitical issues was formalized in 1986 at the Tokyo Summit. Since the Birmingham Summit in 1998, Russia has been actively involved in the group, now often referred to as the Group of 8 (G8). See Stephen Gill, "Group of Seven," in Joel Krieger, ed., *The Oxford Companion to Politics of the World,* 2nd ed., (New York: Oxford University Press, 2001), pp. 340–341.

[32]Stiglitz, p. 12.

[33]Stiglitz, p. 17.

[34]John J. Mearsheimer, *The Tragedy of Great Power Politics* (New York: Norton, 2001).

[35]Mark W. Zacher, "International Organizations," in Joel Krieger, ed., *The Oxford Companion to Politics of the World,* 2nd ed., (New York: Oxford University Press, 2001), pp. 418–420.

[36]Mearsheimer, p. 12.

[37]Mearsheimer, p. 11.

[38]Paul Kennedy, "The Modern Machiavelli," *The New York Review of Books,* November 7, 2002 (http://www.nybooks.com/articles/15803), p. 2.

[39]Mearsheimer, p. 364.

CHAPTER 2

[1]G. John Ikenberry, "Liberal hegemony and the future of the American postwar order," in T. V. Paul and John A. Hall, eds., *International Order and the Future of World Politics* (Cambridge, England: Cambridge University Press, 2002), p. 123.

[2]See Paul Kennedy, *The Rise and Fall of the Great Powers* (New York: Vintage, 1987).

[3]See Michael Cox, "Whatever Happened to American Decline?" *New Political Economy* Vol. 6, No. 3 (November 2001), pp. 311–340.

[4]See: Stephen Gill, "Hegemony," in Joel Krieger, ed., *The Oxford Companion to Politics of the World,* 2nd ed., (New York: Oxford University Press, 2001), pp. 354–355.

[5]It is worth noting that John J. Mearsheimer, one of our four principle interlocutors in the debate on globalization and state power, takes exception to this consensus, arguing in 2001 that the United States is the "most powerful state on the planet" but that it does not dominate Europe and Northeast Asia to the same extent that it dominates the Western Hemisphere and hence does not meet the criterion of global—as distinct from regional—hegemon. In Mearsheimer's definition, "there has never been a global hegemon, and there is not likely to be one anytime soon." See: John J. Mearsheimer, *The Tragedy of Great Power Politics* (New York: Norton, 2001), p. 41.

[6]Hubert Védrine with Dominique Moisi, *France in an Age of Globalization* (Washington, D.C.: Brookings Institution Press, 2001), p. 2.

[7]Védrine, p. 3.

[8]Védrine, p. 44.

[9]Védrine, p. 4.

[10]Thomas Friedman, *The Lexus and the Olive Tree,* updated and expanded ed., (New York: Anchor Books, 2000), pp. xxi–xxii.

[11]In fairness it is necessary to note that Friedman defends himself in a spirited way against those who claim that he is an uncritical advocate of globalization (or for that matter, Americanization). See Thomas Friedman, *The Lexus and the Olive Tree,* updated and expanded ed., (New York: Anchor Books, 2000), pp. xxi–xxii.

[12]Friedman, *The Lexus and the Olive Tree,* p. xix.

[13]Friedman, *The Lexus and the Olive Tree,* p. xix.

[14]*Financial Times,* "Dollar hits record low against euro," November 19, 2003, p. 1.

[15]Ibid.

[16]*Financial Times,* "Washington to place curbs on Chinese exports," November 19, 2003, p. 1.

[17]*Financial Times,* "750,000 US high-tech jobs lost in two years," November 19, 2003, p. 3.

[18]American Electronics Association, "High-tech Industry Sheds More Than One-half Million Jobs in 2002, AeA Report Says" (http://www.aeanet.org/PressRoom/idmk_cs2003_US.asp).

[19]Peter Gowan, "Explaining the American Boom: The Roles of 'Globalisation' and United States Global Power," *New Political Economy* Vol. 6, No. 3 (November 2001), pp. 359–374.

[20]Paul Krugman, "Questions of Interest," *The New York Times,* April 20, 2004, p. A23.

[21]*Financial Times,* "US import curbs come under fire from China," November 20, 2003, p. 1.

[22]*Financial Times,* "Import restrictions risk bitter divorce," November 20, 2003, p. 12.

[23]Tobias Buck, "EU set to hit back at US in trade clash," *Financial Times,* April 29, 2004, p. 3.

[24]Edward Aldeen, "US and China Resolve Trade Disputes," *Financial Times,* April 22, 2004, p. 1.

[25]See Elizabeth Becker, "Global Trade Body Rules Against U.S. On Cotton Subsidies," *The New York Times,* April 27, 2004, p. 1, C12.

[26]See Michael Cox, "Whatever Happened to American Decline?" *New Political Economy* Vol. 6, No. 3 (November 2001), pp. 311–340.

[27]Védrine, p. 3.

[28]Joel Krieger and David Coates, "New Labour's Model for UK Economic Competitiveness: Adrift in the Global Economy," paper presented to the Wake Forest Conference on the Convergence of Capitalist Economies, September 27–29, 2002, unpublished.

[29]Michael E. Porter, Jeffrey D. Sachs, and John W. McArthur, "Executive Summary: Competitiveness and Stages of Economic Growth," World Economic Forum, *The Global Competitiveness Report 2001–2002* (New York and Oxford: Oxford University Press, 2002), p. 17.

[30]Michael Storper and Robert Salais, *Worlds of Production* (Cambridge, Ma.: Harvard University Press, 1997), p. 107.

[31]Peter K. Cornelius, Michael K. Porter, and Klaus Schwab, eds., World Economic Forum, *The Global Competitiveness Report, 2002–2003* (New York and Oxford: Oxford University Press, 2003), p. xiii.

[32]*The Global Competitiveness Report,* pp. 532–533.

[33]Védrine, p. 2.

[34]See Robert Hunter Wade, "The Invisible Hand of the American Empire," *Ethics & International Affairs* Vol. 17, No. 2 (2003), pp. 77–88.

[35]Wade, "The Invisible Hand," p. 80.

[36]See Joseph P. Stiglitz, *Globalization and Its Discontents* (New York: Norton, 2002).

[37]Wade, "The Invisible Hand," p. 82.

[38]Ikenberry, "Liberal hegemony and the future of the American postwar order," p. 124.

[39]Ikenberry, "Liberal hegemony and the future of the American postwar order," p. 126.

[40]See John J. Mearsheimer, *The Tragedy of Great Power Politics* (New York: Norton, 2001), pp. 17–22.

[41]Ikenberry, "Liberal hegemony and the future of the American postwar order," p. 130.

[42]Ivo. H. Daalder and James M. Lindsay, *America Unbound: The Bush Revolution in Foreign Policy* (Washington, D.C.: Brookings Institution Press, 2003), p. 13.

[43]Ibid.

[44]Philip Stephens, "A fractured world remains a very dangerous place," *Financial Times,* December 19, 2003, p. 13.

CHAPTER 3

[1]"Text: Vilnius Group Response to Powell UNSC Presentation on Iraq: http://usembassy.state .gov/islamabad/wwwh)3020802.html

[2]Josef Joffe, "Round 1 Goes to Mr. Big," *The New York Times,* February 10, 2003 (http:// www.nytimes.com/2003/02/10/opinion/10JOFF.html).

[3]United States Department of Defense News Transcript: (http:www.defenselink.mil/news/Jan2003/t01232003_t0122sdfpc.html)

[4]Josef Joffe, "Round 1 Goes to Mr. Big."

[5]Tony Judt, *A Grand Illusion?: An Essay on Europe* (New York: Hill and Wang, 1996), p. 3.

[6]Judt, *A Grand Illusion?,* pp. 3–4.

[7]Huntington, *The Clash of Civilizations and the Remaking of World Order.* It should be noted that Huntington identifies three competing civilizations on the frontiers of Europe (the Christian West, Orthodox, and Muslim); and that for Huntington, the United States and Europe are part of a common Western culture. In the analysis here, I apply the "clash of civilizations" schema differently, emphasizing the Christian/Muslim divide within Europe and asserting (*contra* Huntington) an important U.S./European divide within the West.

[8]Tariq Modood, "Introduction: the Politics of Multiculturalism in the New Europe," in Tariq Modood and Pnina Werbner, eds., *The Politics of Multiculturalism in the New Europe: Racism, Identity and Community* (London and New York: Zed Books, 1997), p. 2.

[9]For a comprehensive and very helpful assessment of Huntington's "Clash of Civilizations" thesis and the important argument that the most basic cultural fault line between the West and Islam involves gender equality and sexual liberalization, see: Pippa Norris and Ronald Inglehart, "Muslims and the West: Testing the 'Clash of Civilizations' Thesis," *Comparative Sociology* (2003) 1 (3–4): 235–265.

[10]Judt, *A Grand Illusion?,* pp. 46–47.

[11]Judt, *A Grand Illusion?*, ch. 2.

[12]Walter C. Clemens, Jr., "Baltic States," in Joel Krieger, ed., *The Oxford Companion to Politics of the World*, 2nd ed., (New York: Oxford University Press, 2001), p. 66.

[13]Tore Bjørgo, "'The Invaders', 'the Traitors' and 'the Resistance Movement': The Extreme Right's Conceptualisation of Opponents and Self in Scandinavia," in Tariq Modood and Pnina Werbner, eds., *The Politics of Multiculturalism in the New Europe: Racism, Identity and Community* (London and New York: Zed Books, 1997), p. 67.

[14]Joel Krieger, "New Labour adrift—the retreat from multiculturalism and multilateralism: A response to Liza Schuster and John Solomos," *Ethnicities* Vol. 4, No. 2 (2004), pp. 295–298.

[15]Elaine Sciolino, "Debate Begins in France on Religion in the Schools," *New York Times*, February 4, 2004, p. A8.

[16]Nora Şeni, "A Recurring Neurosis: Turko-European Relations," in Helsinki Citizen's Assembly, *Modernity and Multiculturalism* (Istanbul, Turkey: 2000), pp. 260–271.

[17]Michael S. Teitelbaum and Philip L. Martin, "Is Turkey Ready for Europe?" *Foreign Affairs* (May/June 2003), pp. 97–111.

[18]Valéry Giscard d'Estaing in an interview to *Le Monde*, quoted in: Michael S. Teitelbaum and Philip L. Martin, "Is Turkey Ready for Europe?" *Foreign Affairs* (May/June 2003), p. 98.

[19]Helmut Schmidt quoted in: Michael S. Teitelbaum and Philip L. Martin, "Is Turkey Ready for Europe?" *Foreign Affairs* (May/June 2003), p. 98.

[20]"Chirac's ruling party opposes Turkey's bid for talks to join EU," *EU Business* (April 7, 2004) (http://www.eubusiness.com/afp/040407165150.sywgk4u6).

[21]Thomas Friedman, "Elephants Can't Fly," *New York Times*, January 29, 2004, (http:// www.nytimes.com/2004/01/29/opinion/29Frie/html).

[22]Thomas Friedman, "Elephants Can't Fly."

[23]Robert Kagan, *Of Paradise and Power: America and Europe in the New World Order* (New York: Knopf, 2003).

[24]Kagan, *Of Paradise and Power*, p. 94.

[25]Kagan, *Of Paradise and Power*, p. 102.

[26]Kagan, *Of Paradise and Power*, p.11.

[27]See Joseph S. Nye Jr., *The Paradox of American Power: Why the World's Only Superpower Can't Go it Alone* (New York: Oxford University Press: 2002).

[28]"President Addresses the Nation in Prime Time press Conference," Office of the press Secretary, April 13, 2004 (http://www.whitehouse.gov/news/releases/2004/04/20040413-20.html).

[29]Ian Burma, "Ties that Loosen," *Financial Times*, January 10/January 11, 2004, p. W4.

[30]Tony Judt, "Anti-Americans Abroad," *The New York Review of Books*, May 1, 2003.

[31]Joel Krieger, *British Politics in the Global Age: Can Social Democracy Survive?* (Cambridge: Polity Press; New York: Oxford University Press, 1999).

[32]Seven Steinmo, "Bucking the Trend? The Welfare State and the Global Economy: the Swedish Case Up Close," *New Political Economy* Vol. 8, No. 1 (March 2003), p. 31.

[33]George Ross, "Economic and Monetary Union," in Joel Krieger, ed., *Oxford Companion to Politics of the World*, 2nd ed., (New York: Oxford University Press, 2001), pp. 231–232.

[34]Will Hutton, *A Declaration of Interdependence: Why America Should Join the World* (New York and London: Norton, 2003), p. 254.

[35]Christopher Allen, "Social Market Economy," in Joel Krieger, ed., *The Oxford Companion to Politics of the World*, 2nd ed., (New York: Oxford University Press, 2001), p. 772.

[36]Christopher Allen, "Germany" in Mark Kesselman, Joel Krieger, and William a Joseph, eds., *Introduction to Comparative Politics*, 3rd ed., (Boston: Houghton Mifflin, 2004), pp. 149–159.

[37]Will Hutton, *A Declaration of Interdependence: Why America Should Join the World*, p. 242.

[38]The discussion of the U.K. economy is drawn largely from previous work. See Joel Krieger, *British Politics in the Global Age: Can Social Democracy Survive?* (New York: Oxford University Press, 1999); Joel Krieger and David Coates, "New Labour's Model for UK Competitiveness: Adrift in the Global Economy?" paper presented to the Wake Forest Conference on the Convergence of Capitalist Economies, September 27–19, 2002 (unpublished, available from the authors); Joel Krieger, "Britain," in Mark Kesselman, Joel Krieger, and William a Joseph, eds., *Introduction to Comparative Politics*, 3rd ed., (Boston: Houghton Mifflin, 2004), pp. 48–50.

[39]Will Hutton, *A Declaration of Interdependence: Why America Should Join the World*, p. 247.

[40]Philip H. Gordon and Sophie Meunier, *The French Challenge: Adapting to Globalization* (Washington, D.C.: Brookings Institution Press, 2001), p.1.

[41]Gordon and Meunier, pp. 35–37.

[42]Robert Graham, "French 35-hour work week loses its allure," *Financial Times*, September 24, 2003, p.1.

[43]Gordon and Meunier, p. 13.

[44]Gordon and Meunier, pp. 13–14.

[45]Storper and Salais, pp. 97–115.

[46]Richard Gordon and Joel Krieger, "Investigating differentiated production systems: the U.S. machine tool industry," *Competition and Change* Vol. 2 (1998), pp. 1–27.

[47]For more detailed analysis of U.K. specialization and competitiveness, see Joel Krieger and David Coates, "New Labour's Model for UK Competitiveness: Adrift in the Global Economy?"

[48]*The Global Competitiveness Report*, pp. 530–531.

[49]Storper and Salais, p. 131.

[50]Storper and Salais, p. 117.

[51]Daniel Hamilton and Joseph Quinlan, "A common interest in prosperity, despite the rhetoric," *Financial Times*, November 17, 2003.

[52]George Ross, "The European Union and the Future of European Politics," in Mark Kesselman and Joel Krieger, eds., *European Politics in Transition*, 5th ed. (Boston: Houghton Mifflin, 2005).

CHAPTER 4

[1]World Bank, *The East Asian Miracle: Economic Growth and Public Policy* (New York: Oxford University Press, 1993).

[2]Shaid Yusuf, "The East Asian Miracle at the Millenium," in Joseph E. Stiglitz and Shahid Yusuf, eds., *Rethinking the East Asian Miracle* (The World Bank and Oxford University Press, 2001), p. 2.

[3]Stephan Haggard, "Newly Industrializing Economies," in Joel Krieger, ed., *The Oxford Companion to Politics of the World*, 2nd ed. (New York: Oxford University Press, 2001), p. 589.

[4]Masahiko Aoki, Hyung-Ki Kim, and Masahiro Okuno-Fujiwara, "Introduction," in Masahiko Aoki, Hyung-Ki Kim, and Masahiro Okuno-Fujiwara, eds., *The Role of Government in East Asian Economic Development* (Oxford: Clarendon Press, 1997), pp. xv–xxii.

[5]Masahiko Aoki, Hyung-Ki Kim, and Masahiro Okuno-Fujiwara, "Introduction," p. xv.

[6]Stephan Haggard, "Newly Industrializing Economies," p. 589.

[7]World Bank, *The East Asian Miracle*, p. 5.

[8]World Bank, *The East Asian Miracle*, p. 10.

[9]Davi Rodrik, "King Kong Meets Godzilla: the World Bank and the east Asian Miracle," CEPR Discussion Paper no. 944, London, Centre for Economic Policy Research, pp. 1–2.

[10]Shaid Yusuf, "The East Asian Miracle at the Millenium," p. 1.

[11]Stephen Gill, "Group of Seven" in Joel Krieger, ed., *The Oxford Companion to Politics of the World*, 2nd ed., (New York: Oxford University Press, 2001), pp. 340–341.

[12]T. J. Pempel, "Introduction," in T. J. Pempel, ed., *The Politics of the Asian Economic Crisis* (Ithaca and London: Cornell University Press, 1999), p. 1.

[13]Donald K. Emmerson, "Indonesia," in Joel Krieger, ed., *The Oxford Companion to Politics of the World*, 2nd ed. (New York: Oxford University Press, 2001), pp. 390–392.

[14]T. J. Pempel, "Introduction," pp. 1–14.

[15]Paul Krugman, "What Ever Happened to the Asian Miracle?" *Fortune*, Vol. 136 (August 18, 1997), p. 27.

[16]Amartya Sen, *Development as Freedom* (New York: Anchor Books, 1999), p. 150.

[17]Mearsheimer, *The Tragedy of Great Power Politics*, pp. 360–372.

[18]Mearsheimer, *The Tragedy of Great Power Politics*, p. 371.

[19]Paul Dibb, David D. Hale, and Peter Prince, "Asia's Insecurity," *Survival* 41, No. 3 (Autumn 1999), p. 5.

[20]Friedman, *The Lexus and the Olive Tree* (2000), p. xii.

[21]For an insightful account of the application of Stiglitz's scholarly work to his participation in economic policy-making and his critique of the IMF, see: Benjamin M. Friedman, "Globalization: Stiglitz's Case," *The New York Review of Books*, August 15, 2002, pp. 48, 50, 52–53.

[22]Joseph E. Stiglitz, *Globalization and Its Discontents* (New York: Norton, 2002), p. 91.

[23]Joseph E. Stiglitz, "From Miracle to Crisis to Recovery: Lessons from Four Decades of East Asian Experience," in Joseph E. Stiglitz and Shaid Yusuf, eds., *Rethinking the East Asian Miracle* (New York: World Bank and Oxford University Press, 2001), p. 523.

[24]Stiglitz, *Globalization and Its Discontents*, p. 93.

[25]Stiglitz, *Globalization and Its Discontents*, p. 73.

[26]Stiglitz, *Globalization and Its Discontents*, p. 73.

[27]Stiglitz, *Globalization and Its Discontents*, p. 99.

[28]For an application of Hegel's observation to East Asian states which prompted the reference to Hegel here see: Meredith Woo-Cumings, "Miracle as Prologue: The State and the Reform of the Corporate Sector in Korea," in Joseph E. Stiglitz and Shahid Yusuf, eds., *Rethinking the East Asian Miracle* (New York: World Bank and Oxford University Press, 2001), p. 343.

[29]Linda Weiss, "State Power and the Asian Crisis," *New Political Economy* Vol. 4, No. 3 (November 1999), pp. 317–342.

[30]See, for example, Meredith Woo-Cumings, "The Political Economy of Growth in East Asia: A Perpective on the State, Market, and Ideology" in Masahiko Aoki, Hyung-Ki Kim, and Masahiro Okuno-Fujiwara, eds., *The Role of Government in East Asian Economic Development* (Oxford: Clarendon Press, 1997), p. 326.

[31]Vivek Chibber, "Building a Developmental State: The Korean Case Reconsidered," *Politics & Society* Vol. 27, No. 3 (September 1999), pp. 309–310.

[32]Meredith Woo-Cumings, "Miracle as Prologue: The State and the Reform of the Corporate Sector in Korea," in Joseph E. Stiglitz and Shahid Yusuf, eds., *Rethinking the East Asian Miracle* (New York: World Bank and Oxford University Press, 2001), p. 359.

[33]Woo-Cumings, op. cit., p. 359.

[34]Weiss, "State Power and the Asian Crisis," p. 319.

[35]Stephen Haggard, *The Political Economy of the Asian Financial Crisis* (Washington, DC: Institute for International Economics, 2000), pp. 137–138.

[36]Yun-han Chu, "Surviving the East Asian Financial Storm: The Political Foundation of Taiwan's Economic Resilience," in T. J. Pempel, ed., *The Politics of the Asian Economic Crisis* (Ithaca and London: Cornell University Press, 1999), p. 187.

[37]Yun-han Chu, "Surviving the East Asian Financial Storm," p. 191.

[38]Weiss, *New Political Economy,* p. 324.

[39]Meredith Woo-Cumings, "Miracle as Prologue: The State and the Reform of the Corporate Sector in Korea," in Stiglitz and Yusuf, *Rethinking the East Asian Miracle,* p. 374.

[40]Cornelius, Porter, and Schwab, *The Global Competitiveness Report, 2002–2003,* pp. 460–461.

[41]Andrew Ward, "International News: growing trade role for north-east Asia" *The Financial Times,* February 11, 2004.

[42]Andrew Ward and Song Jung-a, "Asia and International Economy: S. Korea's new finance minister fires open salvo at foreign-owned banks," *The Financial Times,* February 12, 2004.

[43]Cornelius, Porter, and Schwab, *The Global Competitiveness Report, 2002–2003,* pp. 518–519.

[44]Danial Bogler, "Companies International," *The Financial Times,* March 1, 2004.

[45]The discussion of capacity here draws on Linda Weiss's analysis of "state capacity" and "transformative capacity." See: Linda Weiss, "State Power and the Asian Crisis," *New Political Economy* Vol. 4, No. 3 (November 1999), pp. 317–342; Linda Weiss, *The Myth of the Powerless State* (Ithaca: Cornell University Press, 1998).

[46]Ron Suskind, *The Price of Loyalty: George W. Bush, the White House, and the Education of Paul O'Neill* (New York: Simon and Schuster, 2004).

[47]*Financial Times,* "China must adapt if it is to lead the world economy," November 19, 2003, p. 15.

CHAPTER 5

[1]Jeffrey Sachs, "The world must not let America set its agenda," *Financial Times,* October 15, 2003, p. 13.

[2]Elizabeth Becker, "A World Bank Mission to Bring Help to the Poor," *New York Times,* April 22, 2004, p. W1.

[3]The discussion here of the security threats of the post-9/11 world, the war against terrorism, the role of the Security Council in advancing collective security, and the implications of the war in Iraq closely follow the line of argument in: David Coates and Joel Krieger, *Blair's War* (Cambridge, England and Malden Ma.: Polity Press, 2004), ch. 8.

[4]Michael Reisman, "In Defense of World Public Order," *The American Journal of International Law* Vol. 95, No. 4 (October 2001), pp. 833–835; Jonathan I. Charney, "The Use of Force against Terrorism and International Law," *The American Journal of International Law* Vol. 95, No. 4 (October 2001), p. 833.

[5]George W. Bush, "Statement by the President in His Address to the Nation," The White House, Office of the Press Secretary, September 11, 2001 (http://www.whitehouse.gov/news/releases/2001/ 09/20010911-16.html).

[6]Michael Walzer, "First Define the Battlefield," *New York Times,* September 21, 2001, p. A35.

[7]Michael Howard, "What's in a Name? How to Fight Terrorism," *Foreign Affairs* Vol. 81, No. 1 (January/February, 2002), p. 9.

[8]Radio address: available at (http://www.whitehouse.gov/news/releases/2001/09/20010915.html).

[9]Address to Congress, September 20, 2001, (emphases added): available at (http://www.whitehouse.gov/news/releases/2001/09/20010920-8.htm).

[10]Address to Congress, September 20, 2001, (emphases added): available at (http://www.whitehouse.gov/news/releases/2001/09/20010920-8.html).

[11]Reisman, "In Defense of World Public Order," p. 833. See also Charney, "The Use of Force against Terrorism and International Law," pp. 835–839.

[12]Reisman, "In Defense of World Public Order," pp. 833–835; Charney, "The Use of Force against Terrorism and International Law," p. 833.

[13]Michael Boyce, "Achieving Effect: Annual Chief of Defense Staff Lecture," *RUSI Journal* Vol. 148, No. 1 (February 2003), pp. 31–37: available at (http://www.rusi.org/upload/pdfs/ JA00273-dWopmEK9fx/JA00273.pdf).

[14]Frederic Megret, "'War'? Legal Semantics and the Move to Violence," *European Journal of International Law* Vol. 13, No. 2 (2002), p. 361.

[15]Niels Blokker, "Is the Authorization Authorized? Powers and Practice of the UN Security Council to Authorize the Use of Force by 'Coalitions of the Able and Willing,'" *European Journal of International Law* Vol. 11, No. 3 (2000), p. 541.

[16]Niels Blokker, "Is the Authorization Authorized?" p. 543.

[17]Richard Falk, "After Iraq Is there a Future for the Charter System? War Prevention and the UN," *Counterpunch,* July 2, 2003 (http://www.globalpolicy.org/security/issues/iraq/attack/law/2003/ 0702unfuture.htm).

[18]International Commission on Intervention and State Sovereignty, *The Responsibility To Protect: Report of the International Commission on Intervention and State Sovereignty,* December 2001.

[19]Richard Falk, "After Iraq Is there a Future for the Charter System?"

[20]Chris Brown, "Self-Defense in an Imperfect World, *"Ethics & International Affairs* Vol. 17, No. 1 (2003), pp. 2–16; Richard K. Betts, "Striking First: A History of Thankfully Lost Opportunities," *Ethics & International Affairs* Vol. 17, No. 1 (2003), pp. 17–24.

[21]"Adoption of Policy of Pre-Emption Could Result in Proliferation of Unilateral, Lawless Use of Force, Secretary General Tells General Assembly" September 2003.

[22]"President Bush Addresses United Nations General Assembly," September 23, 2003, (http:// www.whitehouse.gov/news/releases/2003/09/print/20030923-4.html).

[23]Katie Burman, "A Fork in the Road: The United States and the United Nations *"Global Policy Forum *Opinion Forum,* September 25, 2003 (http://www.globalpolicy.org/opinion/2003/ 0925fork.htm).

[24]Ian Williams, "Threading the Needle: UN Resolution 1511 and the Iraqi Occupation," *Foreign Policy in Focus,* October 16, 2003, (http://www.globalpolicy.org/security/issues/iraq/after/2003/ 1016needle.htm).

[25]Blokker, "Is the Authorization Authorized?" p. 541.

[26]Brown, "Self-Defense in an Imperfect World," p. 5.

[27]Robert Keohane, "A Credible Promise to the United Nations," *Financial Times,* March 31, 2003.

[28]Brown, "Self-Defense in an Imperfect World," p. 5.

[29]Adam Roberts, "United Nations," in Joel Krieger, ed., *The Oxford Companion to Politic of the World,* 2nd ed. (New York: Oxford University Press, 2001), pp. 865–867.

CHAPTER 6

[1]Joseph S. Nye Jr., *The Paradox of American Power: Why the World's Only Superpower Can't Go it Alone* (New York, Oxford University Press: 2002).

[2]Edward N. Luttwak, "New Fears, New Alliances," *The New York Times,* October 2, 2002, p. A27.

[3]Lewis H. Lapham, "The American Rome," *Harper's Magazine,* August 2001, p. 31–38.

[4]Wade, "The Invisible Hand of the American Empire," p. 77.

[5]PBS, *The War Behind Closed Doors: Frontline,* "Excerpts from 1992 Draft 'Defense Planning Guidance'," (http://www.pbs.org/wgbh/pages/frontline/shows/iraq/etc/wolf.html).

[6]Jim Lobe, "U.S. Vision of Might and Right Triumphs After 11 September," Third World Network, September 2002, (http://www.twnside.org.sg/title/2399.htm).

[7]George W. Bush, "Remarks by the President at 2002 Graduation Exercise of the United States Military Academy, West Point, New York," June 1, 2002, (http://www.whitehouse.gov/news/releases/2002/06/print/20020601-3.html).

[8]The National Security Strategy of the United States of America (http://www.whitehouse.gov/nsc/print/nssall.html).

[9]Ibid.

[10]Michael Walzer, *Just and Unjust Wars,* 3rd ed., (New York: Basic Books, 2000), p. 76.

[11]John J. Mearsheimer and Stephen M. Walt, "An Unnecessary War," *Foreign Policy,* January-February, 2003, (http://www.foreignpolicy.com/issue_janfeb_2003/walts.html).

[12]Kagan, *Of Paradise and Power: America and Europe in the New World Order,* p. 102.

[13]Michael Ignatieff, "Why Are We In Iraq? (And Liberia? And Afghanistan?), *New York Times Magazine,* September 7, 2003, (http://www.nytimes.com/2003/09/07/magazine/38Iraq.html).

[14]Niall Ferguson, "The Empire Slinks Back," *New York Times Magazine,* April 27, 2003, (http://www.nytimes.com/2003/04/27/magazine/27EMPIRE.html); "Hegemony or Empire?," *Foreign Affairs,* September/October, 2003, pp. 154–161.

[15]Jonathan Schell, *The Unconquerable World* (New York: Metropolitan Books, Henry Holt and Company, 2003), p. 341; see also, Craig Murphy, "Agriculture, Industry, Empire, and America," in Craig Calhoun, Frederick Cooper, and Kevin W. Moore, eds. *Lessons of Empire* (New York: New Press, 2004).

[16]Charles A. Kupchan, *The End of the American Era* (New York, Knopf, 2003).

[17]Wade, "The Invisible Hand of the American Empire," p. 77. Both the name of the thesis and much of the explanation, except where otherwise noted, is drawn from Wade.

[18]Wade, "The Invisible Hand of the American Empire," p. 87.

[19]Stephen Gill, "Hegemony," in Joel Krieger, ed., *The Oxford Companion to Politics of the World,* 2nd ed., (New York: Oxford University Press, 2001), pp. 354–355.

[20]Kenichi Ohmae, *The End of the Nation State* (New York: Free Press, 1995), p. viii.

[21]Michael Mann, "Globalisation as Violence," unpublished paper, UCLA Department of Sociology, (http://www.sscnet.ucla.edu/soc/faculty/mann/articles_site.htm).

[22]Huntington, *The Clash of Civilizations and the Remaking of the World Order,* p. 212.

[23]Ibid., p. 29.

[24]Michael Mann, "Globalisation as Violence," unpublished paper, UCLA Department of Sociology, available at: (http://www.sscent.ucla.edy/soc/faculty/mann/articles_site.htm). Mann includes Benjamin Barber in this characterization along with Huntington and Friedman. See: Benjamin Barber, *Jihad vs. McWorld: How Globalism and Tribalism Are Reshaping the World* (New York: Ballantine Books, 1996).

[25]Ferguson, "The Empire Slinks Back."

[26]Ibid.

[27]Ignatieff, "Why Are We In Iraq? (And Liberia? And Afghanistan?)."

[28]Ibid.

[29]Ibid.

[30]Ibid.

[31]"President Bush Discusses Freedom in Iraq and Middle East," Remarks by the President at the Twentieth Anniversary of the National Endowment for Democracy, United States Chamber of Commerce, Washington, D.C., November 6, 2003, (http://www.ned.org/events/anniversary/ oct1603-Bush.html).

[32]William Safire, "The Age of Liberty," *New York Times,* November 10, 2003, p. A23.

[33]"President Bush Discusses Freedom."

[34]Ibid.

[35]Larry Diamond and Marc F. Plattner, eds., *The Global Divergence of Democracies* (Baltimore and London: 2001).

[36]Minxin Pei and Sara Kasper, "Lessons from the Past: The American Records on National Building," *Carnegie Endowment for International Peace, Policy Brief* 24 (May 2003) (http:// www.ceip.org/files/publications/Pei_PB24.asp).

[37]Vali Nasr, "Lessons from the Muslim World," *Daedalus* 132, No. 3 (Summer 2003), pp. 67–72.

[38]For a very insightful analysis, see: John Langmore, "The Bush Foreign Policy Revolution, Its Origins, and Alternatives," Global Policy Forum (http://www.globalpolicy.org/empire/analysis/).

Index

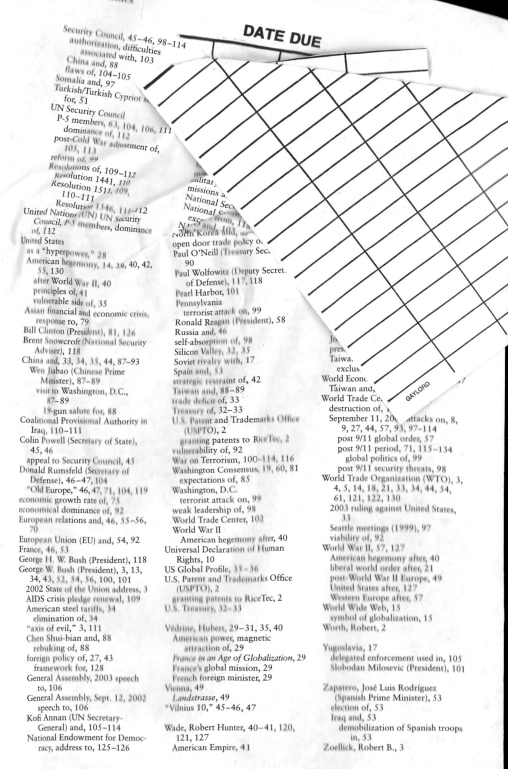

DATE DUE

PRINTED IN U.S.A.

GAYLORD